ISSUES IN THE FUTURE OF ASIA

Issues
in the
Future
of
Asia

Communist and Non-Communist Alternatives

Edited by

RICHARD LOWENTHAL

FREDERICK A. PRAEGER, *Publishers*
New York • Washington • London

FREDERICK A. PRAEGER, *Publishers*
111 Fourth Avenue, New York, N.Y. 10003, U.S.A.
5, Cromwell Place, London S.W.7, England

Published in the United States of America in 1969
by Frederick A. Praeger, Inc., Publishers

Library of Congress Catalog Card Number: 69-19817

Printed in the United States of America

PREFACE: THE LONG-TERM CHALLENGE

The contributions united in this volume concern a number of issues in the struggle for the future of Asia—a number of the factors that may determine whether the most populous continent of the globe will or will not increasingly come under the rule of Communist Party regimes. It does not, of course, aim at offering anything like a comprehensive picture of Asia's problems; nor is it claimed that the aspects treated here will necessarily prove to be the decisive ones. A glance at the table of contents will reveal at once that this book contains no chapter on the war in Vietnam, or on the Chinese "cultural revolution," and the reader may well conclude that a book that discusses the future of Asia without dealing either with the future of Chinese power or with the American effort at the military containment of Asian Communism is like a presentation of *Hamlet* without the Prince. My answer to him would be that the contributors to this volume were seeking to focus attention on some factors that are not so much in the center of current discussion on Asia, yet may prove to be of vital importance in the long run. That, in fact, was the purpose of the small scholarly conference at which the members of the International Research Advisory Council of the Friedrich Ebert Foundation assembled in London in September, 1966, and for which the papers collected here were originally prepared.

The common approach which ties these contributions together, then, is that the problem posed by the conflict with Communism in Asia is not simply that of repelling a military assault, but of responding to a long-term challenge. In a sense, of course, this could have been said about the conflict with Communism everywhere and, in particular, of the postwar struggle for Europe; yet there is a decisive difference of degree. The basic problems of the survival of a free society in the part of Europe that had not been overrun by the Soviet army were problems of reconstruction and revival after the devastations of war and the political and social disruption wrought by Nazi occupation; they could be solved, and were solved, in a comparatively short time, leaving only the balancing of Soviet power as a major long-term issue. But the basic problems of Asia, with the exception of Japan, concern the question whether its nations will successfully accomplish the gigantic task of social, economic, cultural, and political modernization, and under what kind of leadership; and that is an issue the decision of which may well take several generations.

Each of the chapters in this volume is devoted to a different aspect of this process. Werner Klatt discusses the nature of the agrarian problem in Asia, the contributions that Communist and non-Communist programs of reform can offer to its solution, and the political and social pre-conditions for effective reform under a non-Communist regime. One of the most striking conclusions that emerges from his study is that while the reforms devised by non-Communist experts have proved far superior to the prescriptions of Communist ideology—where they have been effectively applied, as in Japan and Taiwan—they, too, imply revolutionary changes in the social structure and have therefore met with tenacious resistance by the traditionally privileged strata of many Asian countries. That resistance has proved particularly frustrating in the largest non-Communist Asian nation, India; and here Dr. Klatt's presentation converges with the analysis that Donald Zagoria offers of the social bases of Communism in that country. Apart from the economic and social problems created by rural overpopulation and its overflow into the cities, these bases turn out to be intimately connected with the persistent conflicts between the various communities, castes, and linguistic groups. It is difficult to envisage how the separatist loyalties underlying these conflicts are to be broken down and replaced by an effective national integration within the existing patchwork of protected group rights, and without the mobilizing effect of a great national movement of revolutionary character.

Both the problem of agrarian reform and the problem of national integration and mobilization thus tend to pose the alternative between hopeless stagnation and a revolutionary solution. Yet, as I have discussed in my own contribution on the problems of economic development, a contradiction may easily arise between the irrational passions unleashed by nationalist revolutionary movements and the need for education toward a Western-type rationality of conduct which has proved a condition for successful economic development. While some of the nationalist movements, as well as Communism of the Chinese variety, appear to have succumbed to this contradiction, Soviet Communism has been remarkably successful in solving it, at least for itself, as was Japanese nationalism at an earlier period. But the very fact that Soviet Communist ideology has accepted many of the goals of Western materialism, as well as the formal criteria of economic rationality, now makes it appear as alien and difficult to assimilate for many Asian nationalist intellectuals as is Western thought itself.

It is in this context that the importance of the indigenous ideological responses of the Asians to the disruption of their traditional society and to the challenge of development becomes clear. Two types of response are discussed on the following pages: the attempts at a synthesis of indigenous religion with socialist programs in modernistic Buddhism are described by Emanuel Sarkisyanz, and the syncretism of a nationalist defense of Asian cultural identity with a modern vision of planning for development and social justice, as conceived by Sun Yat-sen and other Asian nationalists, is analyzed by Gottfried Kindermann. Professor Sarkisyanz' essay illustrates the strong utopian strain in Buddhist socialism—a "peasant utopianism" that has been criticized by Soviet writers as offering a basis for irrational phenomena of the Chinese type.* Professor Kindermann shows how the ambivalence toward Western values—which lies at the root of the syncretistic ideologies—is reproduced in an ambiguity of their political conclusions, which has allowed both the Communists and their opponents to present themselves as the true executors of Sun Yat-sen's legacy. Neither religion nor nationalism, then, is in itself a solid bulwark against the advance of totalitarian Communism in Asia; whether they will prove the alternatives or the pacemakers for the spread of Communist ideology will depend on whether they can be combined with effective non-Communist programs for solving the problems of agrarian reform, national integration, and over-all development.

Seen in this framework, the contest with totalitarian Communism in Asia (and, indeed, in countries with non-Western cultural traditions generally) reveals itself as a long-term challenge not merely to Western power, but to Western civilization. After all, even the totalitarian ideologies and movements that arose *within* Europe had their origin in the strains imposed on the continued growth of that civilization by the process of accelerated and uneven modern-

*See V. Lukin, "Some Aspects of the Class Struggle in South and Southeast Asia," *World Marxist Review*, No. 11 (1966).

ization in its eastern border region, and the horrors perpe-
trated by Nazism and Stalinism in our lifetime have forced us
to realize that the survival of Western civilization was
seriously threatened in its very homeland. But in countries
with non-Western cultural traditions, where the West has
entered as a disruptive force and the beginning of modernization has been due to its intrusion from outside, it is not
merely the capacity of our civilization for survival that is
tested, but its continued capacity for assimilating non-
Western peoples—not in the sense of extinguishing their
cultural identity, but of becoming relevant to their problems.
In that sense, it may be said that the transformation of Soviet
Communism since Stalin's death, though it has brought
neither the end of Party dictatorship nor the end of major
conflict with the Western powers, has meant an important
advance in the evolution of Russia toward a common
civilization with the West. True, contact and affinity between
Russia and the West have for centuries been far more intense
than between the West and those Asian countries that are
now facing their crisis of modernization; but even so, the
recent Russian evolution—the "embourgeoisement" denounced by Mao Tse-tung—would not have been possible
without either the success of Western containment or the
readiness of the Western powers to promote a lowering of
barriers.

The Asian challenge to the West is much harder to meet.
Because the problems of development there arise from a
background of social structures and cultural traditions that
differ profoundly from those known from the Western past,
they will often require radically different institutional solutions; and while Western social science is perfectly capable of
diagnosing the Asian situation and suggesting such solutions,
Western democratic opinion must rise above strong ideological prejudices in order to accept such experiments and
even to support them with aid and advice. Nor is this all: on

the Asian side, the memory of the disruptive impact of Western power and Western capitalist enterprise on these nations is liable to be reactivated by any Western political action taken in support of the vested interests of private combines, and by every display of Western military might on Asian soil; and these memories and actions inevitably reduce the credibility of Western values and of any development programs based on those values for Asian populations—even where those programs are in themselves perfectly suitable for the country concerned. It will not be easy for the governments and the peoples of the West to summon the vision and generosity required for backing, persistently and with the necessary material sacrifices, development policies based on unfamiliar institutional patterns; nor will it be easy for them to understand that, in the long run, the advance of the Asian nations toward modernization along roads that offer effective alternatives to the Communist prescriptions will prove more important than the mere military containment of Communist power. Yet only if the actions of the West are shaped by this kind of insight can Western civilization become increasingly relevant to the Asian peoples. It is on this, I believe, that the future of Asia will ultimately depend.

RICHARD LOWENTHAL

Stanford, Calif.
January 1, 1969

CONTENTS

Preface: The Long-Term Challenge

        by Richard Lowenthal   v

I. Development Versus Anti-Westernism: Russia, China, and the Dilemma of the New States

        by Richard Lowenthal   3

II. The Agrarian Question in Asia in the Light of Communist and Non-Communist Experience

        by Werner Klatt   27

III. The Social Bases of Indian Communism

        by Donald S. Zagoria   97

IV. Buddhism as a Political Factor in Southeast Asia

        by Emanuel Sarkisyanz   125

V. Sun Yat-senism as a Model for Syncretistic Ideologies of Developing Countries

        by Gottfried-Karl Kindermann   149

Notes on the Contributors   177

ISSUES IN THE FUTURE OF ASIA

I

DEVELOPMENT VERSUS ANTI-WESTERNISM: RUSSIA, CHINA, AND THE DILEMMA OF THE NEW STATES

Richard Lowenthal

One of the major factors of instability in the world of the late 1960's is the uncertainty over the political orientation and long-term objectives of the large number of new states that have emerged from colonial status during the past two decades. All of these states look back on a longer or shorter history of Western rule and a more or less bitter struggle by their political and intellectual elites to win independence from the West. All of them owe to the West the ideal of modernization—which to them means chiefly the achievement of material prosperity and power through the help of modern technology—as well as the more or less limited beginnings of the actual process of modernization. All of them are also striving to continue, and to accelerate, this process in a spirit of rivalry with the West; they seek to throw off the alien and cramping influence of the West in order to catch up with it or, to put it the other way around, to take over its techniques of production and organization in order to become independent of it. This underlying ambivalence toward the West, inevitable under the circumstances, is cultural as well as political, for, while the process of

3

technological modernization requires the acceptance of habits of rational thought and attitudes that were first developed in the West, the conscious purpose of the modernizing drive is to preserve, though in a modernized form, the cultural identity of the peoples concerned—the specific character of their traditional values as distinct from those of the West.

The subject of the present essay is the influence that the Soviet Union and China have exercised on the unfolding of the dilemma posed by this underlying ambivalence for the development policy of the new states, and the repercussions that the dilemma has had on the evolution of Soviet and Chinese thinking on the problem of development. Within the scope of this essay, it is of course impossible to give more than a brief outline of the problems involved. But it is hoped that this outline will show that the dilemma faced by the new states between the imperatives of economic development and the ideological passions of anti-Westernism has not only been a major issue in their own political evolution, but has also had an important influence on the growing divergence between Soviet and Chinese policies.

The Early Outlook of the New States

In trying to follow the unfolding of the dilemma, we may take as our starting point the Bandung Conference of 1955. It was at this conference that the governments of Asia, together with a few independent governments of Africa, made their first attempt to define a common attitude in world affairs. If we leave aside the early illusion that the new states, having been born free from the taint of power politics, could place themselves above the conflicts of the Old World and try to arbitrate them from a higher moral plane, and concentrate instead on the hard core of common interests expressed in the debates and resolutions, we find that they revolved around two principal concerns. The first was to protect the newly won independence of the participants against any return of colonialism and to continue—and to accelerate—the process of decolonization until the last dependent peoples had shaken off alien tutelage. The second was to make use of this independence in order to achieve what could not be achieved under colonial rule: planned, all-round economic development, with the aim of bridging the gulf between the industrially advanced minority and the poor, underdeveloped majority of mankind.[1]

In the minds of most, if not all, of the Bandung participants, the relation between these two main concerns was one of interdependence rather than of conflict; imperialist control appeared to them as the principal obstacle to all-round development. Despite the warnings of a few pro-Western governments, the political atmosphere at Bandung was dominated by the view, shared by the neutralist majority and the Communist states present, that the old colonial powers, together with their American allies, constituted the only possible threat to the independence of the new nations; moreover, the privileged positions held by Western business firms in many of the newly independent states were seen as a continuing roadblock to development. Thus anticolonialism and planned development were considered as aspects of a single forward movement by the underprivileged nations, which could achieve their goals of modernization only through repeated conflicts with the Western "imperialists." Yet, to most leaders of the new nations, this concept appeared to be perfectly compatible both with selective imitation of Western models and with reliance on large amounts of Western development aid. In short, while inclined to emphasize the anti-Western aspects of their orientation, the neutralists at Bandung were not yet conscious of a possible dilemma between anti-Westernism and the requirements of economic development; certainly they were not inclined to make a clear choice between the two.

The Communist participants, led by China, were of course much more aware of the implications of anti-Westernism and were correspondingly more willing to advocate a firm commitment to it; but in so doing, they explicitly denied that any dilemma existed. In the years following Bandung, both Soviet and Chinese Communists developed a coherent doctrine according to which the Western imperialists were not only the persistent and insidious enemies of the political independence of colonial and ex-colonial peoples, but also the natural opponents of their economic development. The imperialist powers, by backing the establishment of privileged capitalist combines in those countries, had created the lopsided structure of many of their economies, with their concentration on raw material production and export crops, in order to keep them dependent and exploited; and the imperialist powers would seek to maintain that structure and to prevent all-round development in order to continue to draw profits from these countries, even after the granting of political independence. They would invest capital only to maintain this structure and would grant development aid only to protect the investments of the private capitalists. Hence, all-round development could only be achieved by breaking with the capitalist world market and thus escaping its pressure to preserve the lopsided structure of the underdeveloped countries. Accordingly, the new states would find their only political support for resisting imperialist pressures in the "socialist camp," and their only economic alternative to capitalist exploitation in the "socialist world market" and in development aid from the Communist states. In short, the only road to independent development was the "non-capitalist road," which required a break with the West and economic and political reliance on the Soviet bloc.[2]

To understand the early impact of that doctrine on many of the new states, it is important to remember that there was no lack of illustrations from the actual behavior of Western governments and firms to confirm the Communist theory.

During the Dulles era, the government of the United States tended to use development aid as a means of obtaining alliances and military bases from Asian governments, at a time when the Soviets had demonstratively accepted the right of those governments to remain militarily neutral. The Suez adventure of 1956, organized by the French and British governments in defense of the privileges of a capitalist corporation, would be cited for years afterward as proof that the danger of colonial reconquest was not a figment of Leninist imagination; the conflicts arising from time to time over the rights of oil companies in Iran and Iraq, or of mining interests in Katanga, illustrated the same tendency. Yet, while these events served as fuel for Communist propaganda against the imperialist powers and as confirmation of its thesis that anti-Westernism and independent economic development were simply two sides of the same coin, other developments were gradually undermining that thesis.

The Dilemma Appears

In the first place, experience showed that both Soviet bloc aid and the socialist world market were too limited in extent to make an economic break with the West practicable for the bulk of the underdeveloped countries; there was simply no alternative to Western aid and investment or to Western markets.[3] Secondly, despite the cases of nationalization of Western assets and frequent political conflicts, Western investments in the ex-colonial countries showed a steady tendency to increase. Indeed, the steady growth of Western investments after decolonization is one of the few points about which economic experts on all sides—in advanced and underdeveloped countries, in Russia, China, and the West—are today in full agreement.[4] Thirdly, it turned out that Western governments were not as rigidly committed either to the use of aid as a means of obtaining military advantages or to the protection of the vested interests of capitalist combines as had appeared during the early period of the "aid competition" between the Western powers and the Soviet bloc. The West, and the United States in particular, soon abandoned the Dulles view that nonalignment in world affairs was immoral and reprehensible; the West has come to accept the neutrality of the majority of the new states just as the Russians have accepted it, and to offer them development aid from public funds without pressing for military alliances or bases. Similarly, Western policy-makers have come to recognize that they cannot make the granting of such aid dependent on the internal political or economic systems of the new states—that they will have to aid not only Western-style parliamentary democracies and traditional autocracies but also revolutionary nationalist dictatorships, not only free-enterprise economies but also governments describing themselves as socialist and engaged in a planned policy of development centered on a strong, publicly owned sector. In a number of cases, though not always, Western governments have also continued to offer aid to governments of developing countries that had nationalized the assets of large Western companies, and have even advised these companies to negotiate with the governments concerned in order to smooth the transition. In other words, while there have been repeated cases in which the Western "imperialists" behaved according to the Communist textbook, they have not done so consistently and, indeed, less and less frequently. From the point of view of the developing countries, this has meant that Western aid has not only turned out to be irreplaceable, but that its acceptance has also proved, in the majority of cases, to be compatible with the preservation of real independence in both foreign policy and the choice of their road of economic development.

At the same time, the over-all problems of development were found to be far more difficult than anyone—and the governments of the new states in particular—had expected. It was not only that the total amount of capital aid from all sources, East and West, proved insufficient for the combined needs of industrialization, agricultural modernization, and the creation of a modern infrastructure in countries with rapidly increasing populations; a shortage of capital was by no means the only limiting factor. The obstacles to a concentration on rational economic effort that derived from the inherited social structure and traditional cultural attitudes proved in many cases immensely strong, and the struggle against them difficult and time-consuming at best. The shortage of administrative, managerial, and technical cadres with the necessary skill and integrity turned out to be nearly catastrophic in many new states, and the problem of training sufficient numbers of them quickly well-nigh insoluble, while many new states were threatened with disruption by the separatism of communities based on religion, language, tribe, or caste.[5]

But while the difficulties of development proved unexpectedly serious in all the new states, they manifested themselves with the most devastating effect in those countries that concentrated their main effort on waging an ideological struggle against the West and on exporting their particular type of nationalist revolution. This latter activity, which Professor Hugh Seton-Watson has aptly termed "revolution-mongering," was not, after all, confined to the Communists; for a time it was the favorite occupation of those nationalist leaders who were least willing and able to make the change-over from the struggle for national liberation to the problems of constructive modernization. Inevitably, the countries governed by such revolution-mongering regimes as Ghana under Nkrumah, Indonesia under Sukarno, and, to a lesser extent, Egypt under Nasser had to pay for the glory of playing a role on the world stage with failures of development, because their governments did not have sufficient attention and energy, or sufficient capital and technicians, to spare for a serious effort to deal with the problems of economic development.

In short, it turned out that consistent anti-Westernism, of the kind the Communists had advised and in which some of the revolutionary nationalist regimes had indulged, was incompatible with successful economic construction, which appeared difficult enough in itself. The principle that Sukarno formulated in the classic words "To hell with your aid!" meant, in effect, "To hell with economic development!" The need for a choice between priority for economic development or for anti-Western politics proved to be a real dilemma, and eventually it forced itself on the attention of all concerned. In due course, this dilemma also forced itself on the attention of the Soviet and Chinese leaders, and, once they recognized it, they responded to it in sharply divergent ways and it became one of the major issues dividing them.

Soviet and Chinese Strategies

In order to understand these divergent responses, it is first necessary to look at the different political objectives that the Soviet Union and Communist China are pursuing in the new states and in the underdeveloped world. The Soviet Union appears to be following, in the main, a "strategy of denial" in those areas. Its principal objective, in the short run at least, is not to create more Communist states or more direct power bases for the Soviet Union but to transform regions that formerly constituted secure power bases for the West into contested areas. The consequences of the withdrawal of the former colonial powers from Asia and Africa, together with the growth of anti-Yankee nationalism in Latin America, are to be exploited so as to deny to the Western powers not only the use of these regions as military bases but also the more or less exclusive use of their material resources and their more or less automatic political support. While in most cases the

Soviet Union has little hope at present of drawing these countries into its own sphere of influence,* it would regard its policy as successful if as many of them as possible adopted an attitude of "positive neutrality"—in other words, if they could be prevailed upon to support Soviet policies on a number of international issues.

In concentrating on this strategy of denial, or on winning over the largest number of underdeveloped countries to positive neutrality, the Soviets normally prefer to deal with the existing governments of those countries, many of which offer good prospects for being influenced to the limited extent required. After all, in order to obtain a situation in which an underdeveloped country avoids aligning itself formally with the West and allows itself occasionally to be manipulated, through economic aid and diplomacy, into supporting Soviet policies, it is not necessary for that country to be ruled by a Communist, or even a militant revolutionary, government. This Soviet preference for working whenever possible with the existing regimes in the new Afro-Asian states has led to an increasing Soviet concern with helping those regimes to deal effectively with their problems of development—with promoting their political stability and economic growth. This in turn has led to an increasing sophistication in Soviet expert discussion of the economics of development and to a gradual transformation of the Soviet outlook in this field from a purely doctrinaire and ideological attitude toward a more pragmatic and constructive one. In short, in order to pursue its conflict with the West by means of a realistic strategy, the Soviet Union has begun to influence its friends in the "third world" in the direction of giving priority to economic development over emotional anti-Westernism.

Meanwhile, the Chinese Communist objectives and strate-

*In the last few years, the "progressive regimes" of the Arab Middle East have become an important exception; here, the Soviets are clearly seeking to build up a secure power sphere of their own.

gies in the underdeveloped world have evolved in a radically different direction. The central Chinese interest in the developing countries is not simply to limit the secure spheres of the Western powers by a strategy of denial, but to promote immediate, active conflicts with the West; it is only for the purpose of promoting such conflicts that the Chinese have been and are prepared to offer economic aid to non-Communist countries. Once conflict with the West, or with a pro-Western neighboring country, is present, the Chinese are willing to aid any regime, regardless of its internal character, even if it is a traditional autocracy; in the absence of such conflict, they are not interested in aiding even a revolutionary nationalist regime with "socialist" aspirations. In practice, this has meant that for a number of years the Chinese have been primarily concerned with fomenting outbreaks of anti-imperialist violence in the form of armed risings and "wars of liberation"; Chinese propaganda has stressed this need for violence even in countries that, once having achieved their own liberation, were clearly no longer interested in it. Thus Chou En-lai, during his first journey to Africa, made a major speech about the need for revolutionary violence in Algiers, the capital of a new country that had just emerged from a victorious war of liberation; he was surprised at the lack of response by the Algerians, who were by that time concerned with different problems.[6]

In the course of time, the Chinese naturally discovered that one major reason why many of these countries refused to commit themselves to a consistent anti-Western policy was their interest in receiving a continuing flow of Western aid. Accordingly, the emphasis of Chinese propaganda shifted. Direct appeals for violence against the West were supplemented and in part replaced by denunciations of all Western aid and indeed of all economic ties with the West, which Peking represented as mere means to enslave the underdeveloped nations and keep them at a backward level. Thus, the early Communist thesis of the need for a radical choice between Western and Communist economic ties has received increasingly urgent priority in Chinese Communist propaganda in the underdeveloped world.

When the Chinese found that most of the governments in the underdeveloped world were not prepared to make a radical break with the United States—an insight which their failure to turn the projected "Second Bandung Conference" of 1965 into an anti-American demonstration must have driven home to them—their interest became increasingly concentrated on winning the support of the new revolutionary movements directed against those governments, and also, of course, on aiding and influencing the small number of non-Communist governments that were themselves involved in revolution-mongering. The Chinese were and are looking not for means to promote economic progress in these countries but for means to promote further revolutions—and they do it not out of any illusions about the short-term chances of Communist victories in those areas, but because of the absolute priority they give to a break with the West.

The Revision of Soviet Doctrines of Development

Let us now look at the manner in which the different strategic objectives of the Soviet Union and China have been translated into different doctrines of economic development. The basic fact is that since about 1962, a considerable revision of the Soviet doctrine of development along the "non-capitalist road," as well as of the practice of Soviet economic aid, has taken place. This applies to the attitude toward Western aid, to relations with the "capitalist world market," and even to private capitalist investments; to the relative importance of the growth of heavy industry as against other sectors of the economy; to the pace at which economic diversification at the expense of traditional export

crops is possible or desirable; to the extent to which the
Soviets can enter new financial commitments to these
countries; and to the degree to which they can press for the
adoption of their own road as a model.

To begin with, the Soviet Union has recognized that it
cannot replace Western aid and investments, and that the
economic success of those governments it wishes to back
therefore depends on their receiving aid from the West as well
as from the East. Accordingly, talk about the inevitable harm
caused by Western aid has largely stopped; indeed, the
Russians are now arguing that the victims of imperialist
exploitation have a "right" to obtain aid from their former
masters as a kind of reparation, and to demand that this aid
be given on their own terms.[7] They insist, however, that
acceptance of Western aid is "safe" only for a country under
the firm political control of a "progressive" regime, which can
use that aid in the framework of its own plan and prevent it
from making an impact on its internal structure—as Lenin's
Russia could afford to offer concessions to foreign capital
under the New Economic Policy, because the state remained
in control of the "commanding heights" of economic life.

At the same time, the former doctrinaire emphasis on
giving priority to the creation of heavy industry everywhere,
regardless of the specific conditions in each country, has been
abandoned. Originally, priority for heavy industry had been
urged, as in Russia itself, as a means to ensure full
independence from the imperialists as fast as possible,
regardless of the sacrifices involved. With the recognition
that Western aid will be needed in any case, Soviet
spokesmen have increasingly argued that protection against
imperialist blackmail can be assured by the strength of the
"socialist camp." Accordingly, the arguments for a policy of
balanced growth which, when first put forward by Western
economists, were rejected as devices for keeping the underdeveloped countries in a state of dependency, have in-

creasingly been taken over by Soviet experts as well.[8] In particular, it is now recognized that the forced development of heavy industry may not be feasible for very small countries; that for agricultural countries with a large visible or disguised surplus population it may be more urgent to create labor-absorbing light industries than capital-intensive heavy industries; and that in countries with an acute deficiency of food production an improvement of agricultural productivity may be the most urgent requirement of political stability. Lately, the view that the Soviet Union favors priority for heavy industry in all underdeveloped countries has even been attacked by Soviet writers as a Western slander!

The difficulties of financing rapid economic diversification in countries with a lopsided economy have also come to be appreciated by Soviet experts, particularly in the light of their experience with Castro's Cuba. That experience has shown, on one hand, that a program of diversification may lead, over and above the heavy initial capital investment (which in the Cuban case was financed by Soviet loans), to a permanent increase in production costs, because the import of raw materials for the new industries may prove almost as expensive as the import of the finished products; on the other hand, it has proved that the continuing heavy import budget cannot possibly be met by the developing country if production of the traditional export crop is reduced at the same time (as Cuban sugar production was for some years), because these countries have no other source of foreign exchange. Unless the Soviet bloc were to assume permanent financial burdens quite incommensurate with its economic strength, diversification had thus to be accomplished slowly and without an early reduction in traditional exports.[9]

A few individual Soviet writers have gone even further in this kind of revisionism. Some have argued that in view of the insufficient amount of aid available from public funds, both

Western and Eastern, the developing countries cannot be asked to do without private capitalist investments, and that in certain cases a more cautious attitude toward the expropriation of foreign companies may be part of the price to be paid for economic development. Similarly, some have recognized that in countries where technical and managerial skills are very scarce, a limited number of not-too-powerful capitalist enterprises may be helpful in stimulating development and in increasing the supply of trained manpower. It would appear that these Soviet writers have taken the pragmatic view that a little capitalism is needed to move forward along the non-capitalist road, or to vary an old song, "a little of what you don't fancy does you good."[10]

A final revision of Soviet doctrine, not confined to individual writers but embodied in official Soviet policy, concerns the limitation of the total amount of Soviet development aid. This has shown itself in a growing reluctance on the part of the Soviet and Soviet bloc governments to increase the total amount of their aid commitments, over and above the sums already pledged; in a tendency to confine such new commitments to a few countries where tangible political effects may be expected, particularly in the Middle East; and in a growing preference for "cooperation agreements" dealing only with technical and, particularly, "planning" aid—forms that are far less costly than capital aid but are sometimes very effective in influencing the direction of a country's development.[11]

The new attitude is also reflected in the Soviet government's unwillingness to accept the demands of the underdeveloped countries for a price policy that would in fact subsidize their exports. The complaint of those countries that the secular decline in the prices of raw materials relative to manufactured goods puts them at a disadvantage in the world's markets, and that this form of "non-equivalent exchange" tends to undo many of the benefits they would otherwise reap from development aid, is recognized as justified, in principle, by both Soviet and Western economists, and the Soviets never fail to point out that this handicap of the underdeveloped countries is due to the lopsided structure and low productivity of their economies, which are the result of past imperialist control. But when, at the 1964 United Nations Conference on Trade and Development, the victims of imperialism put forward proposals for a compensatory price policy, the Soviets refused to consider such "leveling" at the expense of their own consumers; the disadvantage of countries with low productivity was an "economic law," and they would not tamper with it.[12]

The basic argument for limiting Soviet aid commitments, as well as for limiting Soviet support for revolutionary movements in the underdeveloped areas, was clearly stated in a *Pravda* editorial published a year after the fall of Khrushchev.[13] Its starting point was the standard formula, coined by Suslov in the course of the polemics with Peking, that the principal international duty of the Soviet Communists consists in building Communism at home—in raising domestic productivity and living standards to serve as an example to others.[14] From that doctrine that "internationalism begins at home," the editorial went on to say that the Soviet Union would, of course, always help its weaker brethren, but only at a limited sacrifice or risk; the basic problems of development, like the basic problems of the struggle for liberation, must be solved by the new nations themselves. But it follows that if the Soviet Union cannot take responsibility for solving the development problems of others, it cannot urge detailed prescriptions for their solution on them either. Limitation of aid implies limitation of influence, and the Soviets have recognized this to some extent. The pluralistic formula that the Soviet Communist Party has come to accept in its relations with non-ruling Communist parties—that "each detachment of the world movement must make its own decisions about strategy"—has now come by analogy to be applied to the friendly governments of developing countries as well.

Of course, the Soviets have not given up the hope of influencing the future course of development in those countries, any more than they have given up the hope of influencing other Communist parties. But they realize that there are limits to the means they can use; they cannot attempt to exercise a doctrinaire control over the development policy of countries that receive Soviet aid, nor to insist on presenting the details of Russian experience as the only "correct" model. Actually, Soviet ideologues appear to disagree about the extent to which the early experience of the Central Asian Soviet republics, and particularly of the Mongolian People's Republic, should be put forward as a model for countries wishing to take the non-capitalist road of development. While some Soviet experts have stressed the different starting conditions in the new countries of Asia and Africa, others still emphasize, as the crucial point of comparison, that those republics could not have succeeded without the protection and guidance of the Soviet Union. [15]

On the whole, however, it now seems to be accepted Soviet policy that each developing country will have to discover the measures that will prove most effective in its particular circumstances. This process of adjustment must, to some extent, be seen as a parallel to the increasing flexibility and undoctrinaire outlook on the Western side. In fact, the adjustment is prompted in both cases by the requirements of a competitive situation. Just as the West has come, in the course of its competition against the Soviet Union, to accept the need for aiding nonaligned, national-revolutionary dictatorships—even when they nationalize Western firms—so the Soviet Union is coming to accept the need for aiding not only nonaligned and non-revolutionary countries, but even countries that depend primarily on Western aid and do not follow the Soviet example in their development policy. The demand of the nationalist leaders of many of the new countries that they be allowed to follow their own road of development— a "third road" between Western capitalism and Soviet Communism—while rejected by Soviet ideologists in theory, has come in fact to be accepted by the Soviet Union as well as by the West.

The Chinese Counterdoctrine

The Chinese, on the other hand, have not only stuck to the original Communist doctrine that the underdeveloped countries must cut their ties with the Western economies as a condition of development, but have elaborated it and made it more rigid in the process. The basic Chinese arguments were summed up in two articles by Kuo Wen, published in June, 1965, in the *Peking Review.*[16] The articles started from the uncontested and striking fact of the steady growth of Western capital investment in the decolonized countries, but only in order to denounce this investment as the biggest obstacle to development. According to the Chinese, Western investments do not only maintain the underdeveloped countries in a state of economic and political dependence on the imperialist powers by conserving their lopsided economic structure; the Western investors are also accused—with the help of some rather odd statistical calculations—of currently taking out of those countries a larger amount in profits than the sum total of aid and investments being put in. This continuing massive exploitation by Western capital is then offered as the principal reason for the widespread failure of development. If the standard of living in the poorer countries is not improving (or at least not improving rapidly), if the gap between the real per capita income of many poor countries and that of the rich countries is still growing, this is due, in the Chinese view, not to the inherent problems of population pressure or to the difficulties of changing the social structure and traditions in these countries, nor is it to be explained by the fact that total aid from all sources is insufficient to cope with the magnitude of the problem: on the contrary, the increase of Western investments is denounced as the principal cause of the widespread failure of development, because it allegedly means an increase of exploitation.

The corollary of this view is, of course, that if the underdeveloped countries were to nationalize all Western investments and to retain all the profits for themselves, they would be able to develop successfully without benefit of any Western aid at all. Thus, while for Moscow increasing economic independence from the West is now merely a desirable *result* of successful economic development, for Peking the immediate and complete elimination of all dependence on Western capital is a *condition* of successful development. The Chinese advice to the underdeveloped countries is to expropriate all foreign capital and to accept no more—not, of course, because the Chinese would be able or willing to replace the West as a supplier of aid, but because the poor countries must rely on their own efforts and mutual cooperation and shun like poison any so-called aid from the rich.

In view of the obvious difficulties that most of the poor countries of the world are bound to experience in achieving economic growth under *any* kind of policy, this Chinese advice amounts in effect to telling them that they should renounce their hopes of material improvement for an indefinite period rather than try to speed it with the help of Western aid. The Chinese are thus coming to be seen in many of these countries as offering not so much an alternative model for economic development as a startling model for "nondevelopment"—for giving absolute priority to the politics of anti-Westernism over the imperatives of economic growth. The course of the Cultural Revolution in China itself has naturally strengthened that impression.

Roots and Prospects

The first conclusion from our analysis, then, is that, underlying the differences between the Russian and Chinese responses to the dilemma of the new states, there is a basically different trend in the evolution of the Soviet and Chinese Communist regimes themselves. In the Soviet Union, the adoption of the new program by the CPSU at its Twenty-second Congress, in 1961, may be said to have marked the triumph of the logic of economic rationality over the logic of ideological dogma—at least in principle. Since then, and particularly since Khrushchev's attempt at a worldwide breakthrough came to grief in the Cuban missile crisis, the Soviet leaders have tended fairly consistently to give priority to the needs of their country's economic growth over the demands of "classical" Communist doctrine.[17]

Conversely, the policy pursued by Mao Tse-tung in recent years—and the Cultural Revolution as its most extreme expression— must be seen as a desperate attempt to prevent a similar triumph of economic rationality over ideological doctrine in China; for it is precisely this triumph that Mao regards as leading to the restoration of capitalism, and against which he warns when calling for the elimination of all "people in authority who are walking the capitalist road." In other words, Mao has decided in favor of a consistent rejection of Western values, which logically includes the refusal to promote in his own country the rise of that Western-invented human type, "economic man," even though in the long run this refusal must prove incompatible with successful economic development.[18] Whether a policy giving such consistent priority to ideology over economic requirements can be continued for any length of time, even in China, is of course an open question. But so long as it determines Peking's official outlook, China will continue to serve as a model for nondevelopment.

Our second conclusion concerns the impact that this divergent evolution of Russian and Chinese policies has had on the new states of Afro-Asia. On one side, the growth of a revisionist theory and practice of development in the Soviet Union has produced a considerable convergence of Soviet and Western policies of development. This convergence is one of means rather than ends—that is, it takes place in a framework of competition and rivalry rather than of cooperation between the Soviet Union and the West; nevertheless, this degree of convergence enables those governments of under-developed countries that wish to concentrate on solving their economic problems to obtain aid from both sides on their own terms and to choose their own road between the blocs with a considerable degree of independence.

On the other hand, the increasingly rigid orientation of China has coincided with the collapse of those revolution-mongering regimes in the underdeveloped world that seemed most willing to join China in giving priority to anti-Westernism over development, and hence with an increasing isolation of China. While the fall of Nkrumah was only of symptomatic importance, the failure of the pro-Communist coup in Indonesia and the subsequent loss of power by Sukarno was a major blow to Chinese plans, not only for a regional bloc in Southeast Asia but for a rallying of the largest possible number of new states in an anti-imperialist front (possibly in the form of a counter-United Nations) under Peking's leadership; Peking's decision, in the fall of 1965, to press for the indefinite adjournment of the "Second Bandung Conference," of which it had been one of the main sponsors, was an acknowledgment of its inability to give such a conference the character it had intended. Even in the Arab world, where anti-Western emotions reached a new high during the Middle Eastern war of June, 1967, the outcome of that war and the increased dependence on Soviet support that resulted are likely to promote a reduced interest in revolution-mongering propaganda and an increased concentration on domestic development, though geared in this case to a forced buildup of military strength under Soviet guidance.

Yet, lest the above outline should encourage a facile optimism about the future of economic rationality and of the Western cause in the underdeveloped world, it must be qualified by a warning. The present isolation of the Chinese and the recent ineffectiveness of their anti-Western propaganda are due in part to temporary causes. The victory of economic rationality in the underdeveloped world is not guaranteed by the laws of history; it will depend on whether rational methods bring better results than ideological anti-Westernism. In view of the objective difficulties of economic development, and of the insufficient amount of aid at present available from all sources, it is by no means certain that rationality will pay off. Should failure occur in many of the countries that are now making a serious effort to concentrate on economic construction, and should it occur on an increasing scale, these states may very well come to despair of ever solving the difficult tasks of development and turn back to an anti-Westernism of the Chinese type. The choice of the new states between priority for development or for anti-Western ideologies poses a dilemma not only for them and for the Communist powers; it is also a test for the West and its ability to contribute to the solution of one of the crucial problems of our time.

Notes

1. See G. M. Kahin, *The Asian-African Conference, Bandung, Indonesia, April 1955* (Ithaca, 1956).
2. For an early systematic statement of this concept, see the report of the Soviet economist G. A. Arzumanyan at the meeting founding the Afro-Asian Solidarity Council in Cairo, in *Conférence des peuples afro-asiatiques, 26ᵉ décembre 1957-1ᵉʳ janvier 1958, principaux rapports* (Cairo, 1958).
3. According to Soviet figures, the total credits for development aid granted by the Soviet bloc and Yugoslavia in the twelve years from 1954 to the beginning of 1966 amounted to 5 billion rubles, or $5.556 billion, *Mirovaya Ekonomika i Mezhdunarodniye Otnoshenya* [MEMO] (Moscow), No. 4 (1966). A Western study by Kurt Mueller, "Die Industrialisierungshilfe des Ostblocks," in *Ostblock und Entwicklungslaender,* Quarterly Reports of the Friedrich Ebert Stiftung, No. 25 (October, 1966), gives the somewhat higher total of $6.288 billion granted by these countries during the same period, and $7.140 billion if Chinese credits are included. By comparison, according to United Nations figures, credits granted by the OECD countries from public and private funds exceeded $8 billion in the single year 1964. Moreover, the actual disbursement of the development credits granted is known to proceed far more slowly in the Communist states than in the West. The most recent Western study, by I. Agoston, "L' aide des pays membres du COMECON en faveur des pays en voie de développement," in *Revue économique et sociale* (Lausanne) No. 1 (1967), estimates that during the eleven years 1954-64, Soviet bloc credits (excluding China and Yugoslavia) amounted to 7.8 per cent of credits granted by the OECD countries plus Japan, while Soviet bloc disbursements reached only 2.4 per cent of the disbursements of the capitalist world. Even if the comparison is made for credits from public funds only, the Soviet bloc proportion rises only to 12.3 per cent and 3.4 per cent, respectively.
4. For a striking Chinese statement to this effect, see Kuo Wen, "Imperialist Plunder, Biggest Obstacle to the Economic Growth of 'Underdeveloped' Countries," *Peking Review* , June 18 and 25, 1965.
5. For a fuller statement of this writer's views on the nature of the problem of development, see Richard Lowenthal, "Government in the Developing Countries: Its Functions and Its Form," in Henry W. Ehrmann (ed.)., *Democracy in a Changing Society* (New York, 1964).
6. For the text of Chou En-lai's Algiers speech, see New China News Agency, December 27, 1963.
7. The point emerges clearly, e.g., in the discussions carried on in MEMO since 1964, particularly in the contributions by G. Mirsky and V. Tyagunenko, and in N. I. Gavrilov's book *The Independent Countries of Africa* (Moscow, 1965). It was recently officially endorsed, with special reference to the pro-Soviet governments described as "revolutionary democracies," by Alexander Sobolev, editorial secretary of *Problems of Peace and Socialism,* at the joint seminar organized in Cairo by this international Communist monthly and the Egyptian progressive monthly *At-Taliah (The Vanguard)* at the end of October, 1966. See Sobolev's report to the seminar in *Problems of Peace and Socialism,* No. 1 (1967).

8. See the discussions in MEMO by G. Mirsky and other contributors, as well as Gavrilov, *op. cit.*

9. For material on the Cuban experience, see Theodore Draper, *Castroism: Theory and Practice* (New York, 1965), chap. iii. For the lessons drawn in the Soviet bloc, see Gavrilov, *op. cit.*, and J. Kuczynski, "Modern Agriculture Under Socialism," *Labour Monthly* (London), February, 1965.

10. See particularly V. Kollontay in MEMO, No. 10 (1965).

11. Evidence for the Soviet effort to reduce the flow of new credit commitments so as to avoid increasing the "backlog" of unfulfilled commitments is discussed in R. A. Yellon, "The Winds of Change," *Mizan* (London), No. 4 (1967).

12. See the Soviet argument in an article by L. Stepanov, in *Kommunist,* No. 14 (1965).

13. "The Supreme Internationalist Duty of a Socialist Country," *Pravda,* October 27, 1965.

14. See Suslov's speech at the Central Committee session of February, 1964, belatedly published in *Pravda* on April 3, 1964. In elaborating the point in October, 1965, *Pravda* quoted a resolution of the Fourteenth Party conference, which, in 1925, had justified the building of "socialism in one country" with the argument that "our success in building a socialist economy is in itself already a powerful factor in the growth of the world proletarian revolution."

15. The latter emphasis is to be found in G. F. Kim *et al.,* "The Theory and Practice of the Non-Capitalist Road of Development," in *Narody Azii i Afriki,* No. 4 (1966), and in G. F. Kim's article in *Pravda* September 14, 1966.

16. Kuo Wen, *op. cit.*

17. For a fuller discussion of this underlying divergence of Soviet and Chinese internal development, see Richard Lowenthal, "The Prospects for Pluralistic Communism," in Milorad M. Drachkovitch (ed.), *Marxism in the Modern World* (Stanford, 1965); and Richard Lowenthal, "Soviet and Chinese Communist World Views," in Donald W. Treadgold (ed.), *Soviet and Chinese Communism: Similarities and Differences* (Seattle, 1966).

18. For this interpretation of the Cultural Revolution, see Richard Lowenthal, "Mao's Revolution," *Encounter* (London), April, 1967.

II

THE AGRARIAN QUESTION IN ASIA IN THE LIGHT OF COMMUNIST AND NON-COMMUNIST EXPERIENCE

WERNER KLATT

Apart from Japan on the Pacific and Israel on the Mediterranean, the countries of Asia are without exception agrarian in character. As Louise Howard said thirty years ago, for millions of persons born in rural districts there is no escape from an agricultural career.[1] This is still the case today, and it will remain true for many years to come. At current prices it costs at least $2,000 to absorb a man outside agriculture. As this outlay often proves too great a commitment, most countries in Asia will not become industrialized as quickly as they desire. They are, in fact, likely to remain predominantly agrarian in character for a long time to come. In spite of increasing industrial production, some are more agrarian today than they were ten years ago. At current rates of investment, it is often impossible to absorb the annual growth of population, let alone to transfer members of the farming community to industry. This is particularly true of China, which has failed in this respect, while at the same time advancing on a narrow industrial front and placing itself, as

27

the first agrarian country in the world, side by side with the industrialized nuclear powers.

The villages of Asia provide the homestead and determine the way of life of at least three-quarters of the population of preindustrial societies, and as a rule more than two-thirds of the working people are engaged in farming. Even so, farming rarely contributes more than half, and often less than half, of the total gross national product. The villages provide a home not only for those who till the land, but also for craftsmen and traders. Frequently, more than one-fifth of the village population is engaged in nonagricultural activities. In the villages can be found the ancestors of the future foremen and managers of factories, of the manufacturers and merchants and of the officers and civil servants of urban, industrialized society. Many nonagricultural occupations are centered in hamlets and country towns rather than in capital cities, which accommodate primarily the administrative, academic, commercial, and military sections of society, but not as yet much industry and industrial labor.

Cities and towns often give the appearance of villages that have burst their seams, without having lost the characteristic features of rural communities. To a large extent they serve as receptacles of rural underemployment without providing urban or industrial alternatives. However much the urban dwellers have turned away from life on the land, they are closely tied in their mentality to the villages from which they are often not more than one generation removed. The towns are the refuge of those who have chosen to escape the villages, where opportunities are limited and life is hard. They attract those with the greatest amount of initiative, but they also accept those who do not fit into any society. They thus provide a home for the innovators and entrepreneurs of a changing society, as well as for its political reformers and its revolutionaries.

An urban middle class is in the making, but it is often not

yet set in its ways. It tends to lack the sense of personal and public responsibility and the individual initiative and readiness to make decisions that are the prerequisites of modern industrial society. Of the urban dwellers, the members of the armed forces are usually among the best trained and the best provided for. They are charged not only with looking after national defense, but also with maintaining law and order in times of crisis; yet they themselves are often subject to the tensions caused by the impact of dynamic industrial change upon a static rural society. The professionals and administrators tend to be weak and inexperienced; yet their responsibilities are often much greater than those of their counterparts in the West. The intellectual leaders of these societies are invariably dissatisfied with the economic backwardness around them and they are impatient for social and political change. The members of the urban middle class are apt to look down on agriculture and to regard industrialization as the remedy for all social and economic ills. They usually see in strong government and in central planning the mechanism by which to fulfill their personal and national ambitions. They like to divorce economic planning from the needs of the rural communities, whose predominance they see as evidence of political dependence, social stagnation, and economic backwardness. They have no sympathy with rural romanticism; nor is there any basis for it.

Characteristics of Asian Village Society

The Asian countryside is as a rule a backwater of development. Subsistence farming prevails, markets are underdeveloped, and the modes of production and distribution have remained almost unchanged for hundreds of years. Often the countryside is overcrowded, but even where the land-labor ratio is not unfavorable, the chief characteristics of preindustrial society apply: high rates of birth and population growth; high incidence of undernourishment and disease;

low mobility of labor and limited nonfarm occupation; permanent underemployment and seasonal unemployment; lack of mechanical power resulting in low yields and low labor productivity; predominance of farm tenancy and fragmentation; low personal and national incomes; exorbitant land rents and interest rates, high levels of indebtedness and low propensity to save, resulting in insufficient investment from public and private sources; and polarization of village society, marked by widespread poverty side by side with concentration, in a few hands, of wealth and income.[2]

This state of affairs has existed for a long time. In spite of increasing physical mobility due to improved transport facilities, village society has often remained frozen. Tribal beliefs and superstitions are never far beneath the surface. Within the village, the expanded family is usually the focus of all activities. Its way of life is strictly circumscribed by the watchful eyes of the village elders, who acknowledge no privacy; and without privacy individual political initiative cannot develop. The village is often dominated by those who own most of the land, money, and processing facilities. They frequently spend as income what should be treated as capital. A growing number of people who are occupied outside agriculture but tied to its rhythm also live in the villages. Unless they conform, they become outcasts. In these conditions opportunities are strictly limited, as are social and economic mobility. Because change means disturbance of the existing pattern, it is suspect. Revelation, rather than reason, governs the relations between man and deity, and poverty is often regarded as meritorious.[3]

In the villages, often over half, and in some cases up to two-thirds, of the cultivated area is farmed by tenants, many of whom have little or no land of their own. They usually have no security of tenure and surrender half of their crops to the landowners, either on the basis of crop sharing or as rent, in cash or in kind. Often no written records of titles or contractual obligations are available. In these conditions the landlord, moneylender, and merchant—at times one and the same person—wield great power in the village. The smaller the farm and the more restricted the choice of crops, the more the grower suffers from these institutional arrangements. The large grower and the specialist have alternative choices from which the smallholder and the subsistence farmer are barred. The latter produce primarily food grains for their own needs and for disposal immediately after the harvest.

There is usually a good deal of disguised unemployment in the villages. Much of it is not expressed in idleness but in the use of insufficient or unsatisfactory tools, which make for low productivity and excessive input of labor. The extent of unemployment is clearly related to the amount of land available and the type of farming. In present conditions, it requires some two hundred working days to cultivate ten acres of land with paddy on wet ground, and wheat, pulses, and oilseeds on dry land. To this must be added the time required to repair the house, the bunds, and the implements; collect firewood and fodder; and carry farm products to the market. This adds up to almost uninterrupted employment all the year around. There is not enough work, however, for the breadwinner and not enough food for his family, if the holding is substantially smaller than ten acres—and this applies in many, if not most, instances throughout Asia; often even five acres is considered a gift of the gods. In these circumstances underemployment and poverty can be averted only if the level of intensity of farming can be raised or supplementary or alternative employment can be found outside farming.[4]

Even allowing for supplementary earnings, total farm income is rarely large enough to provide more than a bare subsistence; sometimes it is less than that. In Asian farming communities, some 75 to 80 per cent of the total net income is often spent on food, the remainder being divided fairly evenly between clothing, shelter, and other daily necessities. Two-thirds to three-quarters of the food bill is accounted for by cereals, which provide the bulk of the daily calorie intake. While the diet is overburdened with starchy foods, its content of animal protein is low. After weaning, the consumption of milk is insignificant. Its absence in the diet of the adult causes shortages of calcium and riboflavin. Where rice is highly milled, the diet lacks thiamin as a result of which cases of beri beri can be found. Short stature, low body weight, and high frequency of stomatitis are the nutritional marks of societies in need of occupational change. Whereas the total food intake is less deficient than is often thought, the evidence of malnutrition is more frequent.[5]

The Pattern of Farming

The pattern of farming, though by no means unalterable, is usually fixed by circumstances. The production of food grains forms the basis of Asian agriculture; all else tends to be of marginal significance, except in the relatively rare cases where the production of a cash crop has led to specialization. While the cultivators are not necessarily hostile to new ideas, most farm operations have not changed for centuries. The art of animal husbandry and grassland farming is largely unknown. Fruit and vegetables take up only an insignificant part of the land used. As a result, the farm pattern, like the diet, tends to be monotonous. The application of modern farm requisites, such as fertilizers, is limited to a relatively few specialized farms. Traditional patterns of crop rotation are rarely questioned.[6]

Within this pattern certain changes do occur, however. In particular, the lines of division between owners, tenants, and laborers are not always rigid. In the rice economies of Asia the farm laborer accounts for between one-third and two-fifths of the total agricultural working population. Owners and tenants often try to maintain their separate status, but any such segregation tends to break down, particularly where the land available for cultivation is limited so that owners and tenants may have to seek work outside their farms to supplement their incomes. There are also agricultural workers who own some land and who thus stand somewhere between the landless laborer and the owner, tenant, or sharecropper. The laborer turned owner is a rare specimen in Asia. Polarization remains one of the characteristics of the Asian village community, except where, as in Japan and Taiwan, it has become more homogeneous as the result of agrarian reform.

The closely knit pattern of Asian village society is broken where plantations have been superimposed on the broad base of subsistence farming. Where plantation crops, such as rubber or tea (or industrial raw materials, such as mineral ores or mineral oils), have led to dual economies, there is usually a basis for prosperity and room for capital investment. In these cases average national incomes are twice to three times as high as in areas of mere subsistence farming. Moreover, plantations, like mineral explorations, have brought a sense of discipline into the conditions of work and an understanding of the money economy, without which industrialization is unthinkable. At the same time, the lack of integration of two basically different forms of farming tends to contribute yet another element of social and economic friction, which becomes all the more intense where plantation labor is provided by members of a racial or religious minority.

If the description of the Asian village community has given the impression of uniformity and monotony, the picture needs correcting; for wide differences do exist. Japan—a group of islands off the shore of Asia, located in the temperate zone, and endowed with a society imbued with a sense of responsibility—has clearly been favored in comparison with landlocked countries that are located in the tropics or subtropics and lack a society accustomed to act from a sense of duty. Countries with a low density of population and a favorable ratio of land to labor are obviously under less pressure than those with a high density of population and an unfavorable land-labor ratio. Countries that are endowed with natural wealth clearly have an advantage over those with few resources. There are also differences in the degree of contact with the West and its effect on Asian society. Countries that have experienced colonial rule or "unequal treaties" react differently to the challenges of development from those that were hardly touched by alien influences. Finally, there are differences in the forms of political leadership and government, ranging from democracies to autocracies, one-party states, and military dictatorships.

The list of instances in which special factors are at work could easily be extended. This applies in particular to differences in cultural background and institutional arrangements. In view of the differences in geographical, climatic, historical, cultural, and other respects, the similarity in the conditions of preindustrial Asian societies is all the more significant; most striking of all are the similarities in the agrarian pattern and the problems that arise from it.

Communist Patterns of Agrarian Policy

In their search for solutions to the problems of development, the leaders of Asian countries tend to display an understandable uncertainty. The expert advice that is frequently given without sufficient respect for the complexity of the Asian scene has not endeared the representatives of foreign agencies to the political leaders and economic planners in Asia. Fascinated by, yet critical of the Western way of life, they are prepared to consider any alternatives that offer themselves. Among them, the Soviet and Chinese patterns of development have their special attractions. The Communist pattern of agricultural policy still arouses interest, in spite of its notorious failures. This interest is borne out by the reports of such fact-finding missions as those sent in the 1950's from India to China. There is more than one reason for this readiness to consider Soviet or Chinese alternatives.

When looking at Soviet-type societies, the leaders of developing countries in Asia, as in Africa, are acutely aware of an affinity of approach and purpose that they often find lacking in the industrialized West. In spite of their recent industrial achievements, Russia and China are very much closer than the industrialized societies of America and Europe to the agrarian communities of Asia. As any traveler in Communist countries who has an eye for processes of social and economic change will confirm, the gap between industrial advance and agricultural stagnation is staggering.

As late as 1961, the number of urban dwellers in the Soviet Union was no larger than the population living in villages; at that time approximately two-fifths of the working population was engaged in agricultural pursuits, producing, at best, a rather meager diet. In fully industrialized countries, one-tenth of the total working population usually produces all the ingredients of a highly sophisticated diet for the whole nation, and sometimes more than is needed to meet domestic requirements. In these conditions, the outlook of the society is urban in all essentials. In the Soviet Union, the characteristics of rural society are still readily discernible in all walks of life. The backwardness of the rural areas has left its mark. Not unnaturally, Soviet advisers are less surprised than their Western counterparts when they face the shortcomings of Asian communities.

Conditions in China are even closer than the Russian to those in non-Communist countries of Asia. At least four-fifths of China's population still live in villages, and at least

70 per cent of the working population is directly engaged in farm work. The agricultural sector probably accounts for approximately two-fifths of the nation's total output, and grain, the basis of all farming, provides as much as one-fifth. Furthermore, almost half the state budget originates in the direct and indirect contributions of the cultivators. Finally, in spite of large-scale imports of grain in recent years, agriculture continues to be the largest single contributor to the country's export trade. The pre-eminence of the agrarian aspect is equally plain in the social and political sphere. In China, as elsewhere in Asia, the structure of the village community and the development of the farming industry are thus of crucial importance.

Yet, in the Soviet Union and China—as in the non-Communist countries of Asia—the political leaders, in spite of recent concessions to the farming community, consider industrialization as a panacea and the central industrial plan as the chief instrument of development. It took England more than one hundred years to grow from the early beginnings to the heights of capitalism, and Japan had approximately fifty years to turn into a modern industrial nation. Against this, the Soviet Union claims to have achieved this in less than three decades.[7] China appears to have moved with breathtaking speed from the stagnation of a frozen society to a state of industrial development.

Soviet and Chinese publicists have been skillful in withholding the fact that these claims do not take into account some vital aspects of development. In fact, Soviet Russia started, at the beginning of the First Five-Year Plan, from a far higher level of development than exists in most developing countries today. As to China, present steel production per capita equals one-thirtieth and one-fortieth, respectively, of steel output in Britain and in the United States; and China's current per capita supply of energy from all sources provides a mere 6 per cent or so of the amount available in Britain.

In measuring the degree of success or failure of Communist farm policies, we can rely upon original sources to a much greater extent than in the past. Even the most searching Western analysis[8] has been dwarfed by the statements of Communist leaders. In the Soviet Union, the concern of the leadership for the state of farming is reflected by the frequency with which it is discussed at Party meetings. During the Krushchev era, it appeared on the open or secret agenda of almost every meeting of the Central Committee. Since his departure from the political scene, it has continued to receive the full attention of the Soviet leadership. Yet the breakthrough to success is far from certain. From Lenin to Brezhnev, Soviet leaders have never understood the role of farming in a modern society; they have not mastered the art of integrating the rural sector into an increasingly urbanized society; nor have they succeeded in bringing the farming industry into line with the rapidly developing industrial sectors of the national economy.

Soviet Agricultural Policies

Lenin, the strategist of the October Revolution, never abandoned his preference for large-scale communal agriculture over small-scale individual farming, except when, in 1917, the success of the Bolshevik Revolution appeared to depend upon the support of the peasants. At that point he shelved his own Party's program and adopted, as a temporary expedient, the agrarian program of his chief rivals in the struggle for power. Thus, the distribution of land to returning soldiers and landless tenants became one of the main demands of the revolution. The reamalgamation of small farms into large collectives remained the ultimate aim, but the creation of collectives was deferred until after the consolidation of power. A few years later, Lenin chose, once again, the pragmatic decision in preference to the Party dogma. When the sailors of Kronstadt mutinied and demanded, *inter alia,* the right of the peasants to keep their own livestock and to farm their land as they pleased, Lenin abolished the system of requisitioning and allowed, as a temporary expedient, the free sale of agricultural produce after payment of tax in kind.

Within a few years of Lenin's death, Stalin—having liquidated the opposition of Bukharin and others—returned to the dogma that had been temporarily abandoned by his predecessor. On the eve of World War II, hardly any land remained in private hands. The opposition of the peasants had been broken, large-scale deportations had taken place, and irreparable damage had been done to farming. Even within the framework of the collectives, the peasants continued to be treated as enemies of the state rather than as vital members of a new industrial society.

Twenty-five years later, at the time of Stalin's death, farming was where it had been in the days of the Tsars. Admittedly, horses had been replaced by tractor power so as to free acreage under animal fodder for the production of food, but even these modest results had been achieved only at great cost in men, beasts, and materials. The results were particularly disappointing in livestock farming. The number of productive livestock was one-tenth smaller than it had been before collectivization. In the meantime, the human population had grown by almost one-fifth. Milk yields and carcass weights, like grain yields, had remained unchanged. As a result, the nation's diet was smaller in volume and poorer in composition in 1953 than it had been a quarter of a century earlier. The farming community was much worse off than it had been before collectivization. Whereas industrial production had fully recovered from the devastation caused by the German invasion, the supply of farm products continued to lag behind. The cleavage that had been created when forced industrialization and collectivization had driven the two sections of Soviet society apart in the early 1930's had widened rather than narrowed.

The ten years of Khrushchev's rule were largely taken up by attempts to remedy the situation. During this time he made nearly two hundred speeches concerned exclusively with agriculture. Every year, the leader of the world's second largest industrial nation spent a month touring the countryside, criticizing shortcomings and suggesting remedies. Yet, when he was removed from power, his successors had nothing good to say about his agricultural policy. Posterity is likely to be more impartial and to balance his failures against his achievements. There were many of both. In the technical sphere, Khrushchev started three major campaigns; the reclamation of the virgin lands of Central Asia; the introduction of maize as a feed grain and a green fodder; and the abolition of ley farming, i.e., putting grassland under the plow.

At the same time, major changes were made in the administrative sphere. These included the abolition of the machine tractor stations—once considered an essential ingredient of collectivized agriculture—and the transfer of the equipment to the collectives. Khrushchev also eliminated the agricultural ministries as controlling organs of the farm industry and limited their responsibilities to research and advisory services. Finally, he divided the Party along "lines of production," with the object of involving the Party directly in the affairs of the countryside. Much of this was done in a highly unorthodox manner, and some of it was undone when it proved impracticable.

There were also major innovations in the economic sphere. Farming, which for a quarter of a century had been the chief, if not the only, source of capital accumulation for investment in industry, was granted a growing portion of the exchequer's funds. Moreover, increases in farm prices and agricultural wages and reductions in taxes and delivery obligations resulted in an increase of 50 per cent in the disposable income of the farming community. Since one quarter of the collective farmer's cash income had to be reinvested, rural living standards in 1963, though improved by comparison with the dismal level attained in '1953, were still substantially below those of the industrial workers, who in turn had a considerably more modest standard of living than their counterparts in Western industrialized society.

The technological changes also yielded only limited results. The extension of the acreage in Central Asia resulted in a substantial, though precarious, addition to the supply of grain. When the reserves of the soils in Kazakhstan were exhausted, the effects were most damaging. The maize campaign provided supplementary fodder for the dairy herds; but the maize silage failed to provide the plant protein badly needed in the production of animal protein. The plowing up of grassland was designed to remedy this shortcoming, but it was denied its full success because of the lack of fertilizers. The crop failure of 1963, which necessitated a cut in the number of pigs by 30 million, or over 40 per cent, and an import of 10 million tons of grain—an all-time record—was nature's revenge for the mistakes committed in the past. It showed how vulnerable Soviet agriculture remained, in spite of all the improvements made during a decade in which farming received more public recognition than at any other time since the October Revolution.

Whenever technical or economic measures proved to be insufficient, Khrushchev turned to organizational remedies and relied on the lead that the Party cadres were supposed to provide throughout the countryside. He never recognized the fundamental errors underlying the Party doctrine; or, if he did recognize them, he was unable or unwilling to draw the necessary conclusions. He committed his most serious error when—on doctrinal grounds—he began to interfere with the private plot, the only sector of the farm economy that could claim satisfactory results.

To sum up, the ten years of farm policy under Khrushchev yielded an increased, though precarious, supply of food and fodder, without getting anywhere near the ambitious targets set for 1965. The diet, still overburdened with carbohydrates and short of animal proteins, continued to lag behind that of the United States, which for ten years had provided the yardstick for the Soviet Union. The lag proved to be particularly great with regard to the labor requirements of agriculture. In Khrushchev's own assessment, the Soviet Union required five to seven times as much labor as in the United States in arable farming and up to sixteen times as much in livestock farming. At the end of Khrushchev's rule, the pattern of farm productivity, as of food consumption, was still that of a backward country. Yet, in the industrial and military sphere, Russia could legitimately claim to be the second most powerful nation in the world.

There is no reason to think that this dichotomy will disappear as a result of the policy of consolidation, following a temporary retrenchment, on which Brezhnev and Kosygin, men of greater caution than their predecessor, have embarked. Although realism and hesitation are seemingly taking the place of the irrationalities and ambitions of the past, there remains a serious lack of understanding of the role of agriculture in the national economy and of the place of the farmer in modern society. Basically, the erroneous views of the past persist, and the peasants continue to be regarded as politically expendable, even if—as a matter of expediency— they are temporarily treated with more concern than in the past.[9]

Many of the measures taken by the new leadership amount to a continuation of Khrushchev's policies—by different means. Others are of an altogether different nature. The gradual introduction of a guaranteed monthly pay for members of collectives, at rates corresponding to those awarded on state farms, is the most important innovation of the new leadership. If this promise is kept, it ought to remove one of the chief grievances of the collective farmer. One major promise has yet to be fulfilled. The third Kolkhoz Congress, originally scheduled for early 1959, has still not taken place. If the liberal critics of present farm policies gain ground, substantial improvements in the structure and performance of agriculture ought to result. If the traditionalists hold their ground—and this seems more probable under present conditions—no startling changes are likely to occur. The new leaders, like their predecessors, have shown no sign yet of wishing to interfere with the agricultural structure or the pattern of farm operations.

China's Agricultural Policies

On the face of it, China's agricultural policies seem largely to conform to the Soviet pattern. It would be an over simplification, of course, to suggest that all that has occurred in the Chinese countryside has been only a repetition of what had previously happened in Russia. China's agrarian pattern and its mode of farm production differ too much from conditions in the Soviet Union to permit any sweeping generalizations. The high density of China's village population, the close ties of the rural family, and the special features of wet farming must have presented the Chinese Communist leadership with problems that were absent in the Soviet Union. Mao in China—like Lenin, Stalin, and Khrushchev in Russia—made his own contribution to Communist theory and practice. But in spite of such specifically Chinese phenomena as the communes, in essentials the Chinese way of dealing with the rural communities and with farming has been remarkably reminiscent of the Soviet pattern. This applies, in particular, to the distribution of land to small owners, tenants, and landless laborers in the early phases of the revolution, followed by the concentration of individual plots in mutual aid teams, which were soon turned into "producers' cooperatives" and, finally, into communes.[10]

In view of the peculiarities of the Chinese scene, the similarity between the Chinese and the Soviet treatment of the agrarian problem is startling. It is explicable only in the light of an approach that is common to Communist regimes wherever they gain control. Unless this basic identity of Chinese and Soviet agrarian policies is understood, the Chinese pattern may well be accepted where the Soviet variant is regarded as inapplicable in Asian conditions. This is, in fact, a thought that the Chinese Communists have been anxious to convey to Asian leaders. The Sino-Soviet dispute over matters of Communist doctrine and national interests has given China opportunities that did not exist in the past.

Agrarian reform in China was carried out on a nationwide scale only after the Communists had seized power. The main purpose of the agrarian reform law of 1950 was the confiscation and redistribution of the landlords' property. It led to the destruction of the only effective authority, outside the Communist Party, in the villages, which as a result of the reform were divided against themselves.[11]

The reform was carried out with more than the "little terror" that Mao had favored. It took place in four stages. In the first, the villagers were induced by Party cadres to take action; in every village "struggle meetings" were held at which landlords were identified, accused, often beaten up, and sometimes executed on the spot. During the second phase, the class status of the remaining members of the village community was determined. Thereafter, land and property were confiscated without compensation. Finally, old title deeds were destroyed and new landholding certificates issued.

The confusion that developed as the result of arbitrary

measures, including wrong classification, was on a large scale;
so was the demoralization caused by denunciations and other
revolutionary excesses. At the same time, there must have
been a considerable amount of satisfaction, since almost 50
million hectares (125 million acres), taken from some 4
million large landowners, were distributed among almost 50
million households of smallholders, landless peasants, and
farm laborers. Half the number of farming households thus
benefited. As a result of this reform, large landowners very
nearly disappeared, while middle peasants dominated the
village scene. Since the large landowners had often also been
merchants and moneylenders, the state had to step in and
take over their functions, i.e., to collect and sell the farm
surplus, provide credit facilities, and, last but not least,
impose levies.

The Chinese Communists had so far closely followed the
Soviet precedent, and in spite of protestations to the
contrary, the road from land reform to collectivization
seemed a foregone conclusion. In the initial period, the
cultivators were induced to join mutual-aid teams, the lowest
stage of so-called "cooperatives," and they were assured that
the principle of "voluntariness" would be respected, though
landlords and rich peasants were refused admission to the
cooperatives. The Draft Constitution, endorsed by the
National People's Congress in 1954, provided for the promotion of producers' cooperatives as the principal means for the
transformation of individual farming into collective ownership. Full collectivization was set in motion following Mao's
report in July, 1955, "On the Cooperatization of Agriculture." By the end of 1957, collectivization had been
completed for all practical purposes, except in some hill
areas. It was, of course, collectivization without mechanization. The plan to collectivize half the peasants by the end
of 1958 had thus been overfulfilled by a process of

persuasion applied on a gigantic scale. Payment was no longer based on land, but exclusively on labor.

During the next phase, the Chinese cultivators were organized in communes before they had fully recovered from the shock suffered during collectivization. Within a period of six months, 100 million peasant families abandoned a way of life which for centuries had been a part of China's tradition. The People's Communes were supposedly created in compliance with the enthusiastic demands of the mass of the peasants. In fact, since collectivization had destroyed the village community as an operative social and administrative entity, the cultivator had ceased to have a will of his own. He now paid the price for having associated himself with the Party cadre in the struggle against members of his own community. The price was loss of freedom within the family, on the farm, and in the village.

From the summer of 1958 to the end of the year, some 750,000 collectives were merged into 26,000 communes. The collectives had controlled, on the average, some 150 families. Now each commune was responsible for some 5,000 families. It was charged with feeding, housing, and educating the men and women in its care, as well as directing them to communal places of work and training on farms and roadsides, in industrial establishments and paramilitary organizations. This was the most momentous experiment in social engineering that has been recorded in modern history. As was to be expected, it failed; and with it failed the Great Leap Forward, with which the Chinese leaders hoped to raise the country, in one great swoop, from a state of agrarian backwardness to one of modern, industrial development. By 1961 the communes had ceased to operate as central organs of control; they were reduced to accounting agencies.

Within agriculture, the Great Leap Forward was to be achieved as a result of a Twelve-Year Plan, which was first introduced at a Supreme State Conference held in January, 1956, later revised on points of detail, and approved in its third draft by the National Congress of the CCP in May, 1958. It was formally adopted by the National People's Congress in April, 1960, when the failures of the communes and the Great Leap Forward had already become public knowledge both in China and abroad. The Twelve-Year Plan envisaged a grain output of about 450 million tons by 1967, as against a harvest of little more than 180 million tons in 1955. This and other related targets were to be achieved as the result of simultaneous improvements over a wide field, with the aid of fertilizers, irrigation, flood control, mechanization, pest control, high quality seed, land reclamation, and multiple cropping. The results were expected—wrongly—to accrue from the cumulative effects of these measures, instead of being regarded as interdependent. The plan came to naught. By 1965, farm production was scarcely any larger than in 1957, the last year before the gigantic experiments started; but the population that had to be fed had increased by close on 100 million people.

The nation paid dearly for the folly of its leaders, who blamed the vagaries of nature rather than themselves. (An editorial published in the *People's Daily,* on January 1, 1966, belatedly admitted certain errors that had been committed in the years following the Great Leap Forward.) In the meantime, the nation had endured three years of bad harvests and insufficient grain supplies, during which the average food intake declined to approximately 1,850 calories a day, causing loss of body weight, retarded growth among children, and reduced output among working men and women.

In the inner-Party controversy that these developments provoked, the moderate wing of the Party eventually gained a partial victory over the extremists, and early in 1962 farming was given pride of place in economic planning and investment policy. The cultivators were allowed to engage in "sideline production" on their private plots and to sell their produce in markets free of government control. The recovery of farm output was instantaneous, but by the end of 1965, grain production was no larger than in 1957 and the population was still short of foodstuffs. In spite of a regular annual import of approximately 5 million tons of grain and flour, the diet continued to provide no more than 2,000 calories a day, as against 2,200 calories at the time of the Japanese invasion in 1931.

It is worth remembering that the defunct Twelve-Year Plan for agriculture had called for an output of almost 450 million tons of grain—as against a probable crop of, say, 185 million tons. China's agriculture has, of course, some substantial untapped reserves, but as long as fertilizer supplies are only large enough to meet part of the commercial and none of the grain crops, the shortages in basic foodstuffs are bound to remain. Mechanized irrigation facilities also fall far short of actual needs. Since China has once again entered a revolutionary phase, in the course of which, in the Chinese phrase, politics has taken command over economics, only modest improvements of farm output and food consumption should be expected during the current Five-Year Plan period. For the time being, nature, rather than man, determines the level of farm production. Since man's interference often proves detrimental to output, the growth rate of farm production may not exceed that of the population. It may even lag behind it.

Methodological Errors

In China, as in Russia, realism and caution for a time took the place of the former irrationalities and ambitions, but a return to a more rigid interpretation of the doctrinal concepts cannot be ruled out. In China, the "Great Proletarian Cultural Revolution" has, indeed, led to a new phase of political rigidity. As long as the errors on which Communist agrarian policies are based remain uncorrected, the Communist leaders find themselves in an impasse. They have inherited from their political tutors a highly misleading theoretical background and no practical guidance, and they themselves have contributed little to clarify the situation in either a theoretical or practical way.

The founders of Marxism failed both to find a place for the agrarian scene in their criticism of the past and to integrate it into their vision of the future. Contrary to their expectations, Communism failed to gain power in the industrial countries of Western Europe. Instead, Communists succeeded in seizing power only in countries predominantly agrarian in structure, underdeveloped in their economic and social infrastructure, and backward in their industrial makeup. Marx had only the vaguest ideas about the role of agriculture in modern society. He anticipated that here, as in industry, large-scale enterprises would destroy "the bulwark of the old social order, the peasant," but he did nothing to examine the function of peasant farming under capitalism. Toward the end of his life he became painfully aware that his treatment of the agrarian question left much to be desired. His followers were perturbed by this state of affairs, but they failed to clarify the position. They considered farming the most primitive mode of production and the farming community the most backward section of society; yet they realized that without the rural vote they might never become politically effective.

Engels, Marx's closest collaborator, warned in his study *The Peasant Question in France and Germany* that "it is not in our interest to win the peasant overnight only to lose him again on the morrow if we cannot keep our promise."[12] This was written in 1894. Today it reads like a prophecy of what happened a quarter of a century later in Russia and half a century later in China. It has remained one of the mainstays

of Marxism that small-scale farming is economically backward and that the peasant-cultivator is tied to the reactionary
political forces siding with the bourgeoisie rather than the
revolutionary spearhead of the industrial working class.
Whereas the peasant-cultivator is supposed to be committed,
by virtue of his property, to the capitalist cause, his pattern
of production is considered that of the working class. He is
therefore thought to have a conflict of interests and loyalties
that prevent him from joining the forces of the revolution. In
the Marxist view it therefore falls upon the industrial working
class to take the lead on the road to economic progress
through large-scale farming and to political emancipation
through the alliance between industrial workers and peasant-
cultivators.

The followers of Marx and Engels also considered farming
the most primitive form of production and the farming
community the most backward sector of society, vacillating
between capitalism and socialism. Lenin formulated this view
later in these words: "The peasant as a toiler gravitates
towards socialism and prefers the dictatorship of the workers
to the dictatorship of the bourgeoisie. The peasant as a seller
of grain gravitates towards the bourgeoisie, to free trade, i.e.,
back to the 'habitual' old 'primordial' capitalism of former
days."[13] At the same time, Marxists felt the need to enroll
the rural population as supporters of their cause and thus to
come to terms with them. The dilemma that haunted the
early Russian Marxists in their relations with their opponents,
the Narodniki, and took them to Engels with a request for
intellectual help, also marked the later debates of the Social
Democrats and social reformers in various countries of
Europe.

Even as astute a critic of Lenin and the Russian Revolution
as Rosa Luxemburg remained confused when it came to
judging the agrarian question. She regarded the distribution
of the land to the peasants as an ill-considered departure

from the road to socialism and observed that "Lenin's agrarian reform created a new and powerful layer of popular enemies of socialism in the countryside." Yet, at the same time, she spoke with envy of the "French small peasant who became the boldest defender of the French revolution and as Napoleon's soldier carried the banner of France to victory and smashed feudalism in one country after another."[14] Like others before and after her, she remained a captive of an error of Marxist analysis that has haunted Communists to this day.

The indecisions and vacillations left their mark on the European political scene, no less than on those whose fate was in dispute. In the revolutionary upheavals of 1848, the peasants and their representatives did not take sides between the contending parties. Later, they were antagonized by the attitude displayed by the political leaders of the new working-class movements. The contrast between peasant and working-class leaders was particularly pronounced in countries with large rural populations, such as Tsarist Russia and the Balkan states. In spite of this predicament, Communism succeeded in bringing about profound social change, where radical and social reformers had failed. There remained the conflict, however, between the necessity of gaining the support of the peasants in a revolutionary situation and the ultimate aim of eliminating the peasants as a factor in the political and economic life of the country. This problem has dominated the Soviet scene ever since Lenin decided in favor of temporary expediency on his arrival in Petrograd in April, 1917. The conflict has loomed large in nearly every internal purge of the Party from Stalin's struggle against Bukharin to Khrushchev's removal from power. Time and again the losing faction has been accused of, or has had to confess to, misjudging the political position of the peasant and the economic role of agriculture under Communism. The conflict between the doctrine and its practical application must also be regarded as ultimately responsible for the Chinese Communists' misconception of the Great Leap Forward and for the failure of the communes. That the agrarian question features prominently on the agenda of almost every session of the Central Committee of the CPSU and the congresses of the Chinese Communist Party is an indication of the failure to find a solution that would bring into harmony the doctrinal concept and its practical implementation.

Basically, the erroneous views of Marxism persist. Small-scale farming, as defined by Marx, is still regarded as economically backward, and the peasant cultivator is thought to be tied to reactionary forces hostile to the industrial working class. Private farming, though no longer discouraged in Russia and Eastern Europe to the same extent as in the past, remains limited to small plots and small numbers of livestock. As a matter of political philosophy, preference continues to be given to farming in large units and under strict public direction, either in state farms under government management and farmed by workers, or in collectives also run by government appointees and without the active participation of the members of the collectives. These institutional arrangements have a detrimental effect on individual initiative in the public sector, and they are responsible, more than anything else, for the continually unsatisfactory state of the farming industry.

The confusion that has bedeviled Marxist views on the role of different farm sizes for almost a hundred years has yet to be cleared up. If performance in farming were measured in the same way as in industry, farms that are small in terms of acreage would often be found to be large enterprises when considered in terms of capital input and output per man. In other words, it is the degree of intensity that matters, not the acreage. This interrelation between size in terms of acreage and intensity has never been understood by any of the Communist leaders. (This does not, of course, dispose of the need to consider economies of scale within each type of farming.)

Nor is it fully recognized in Communist countries that farming, unlike industry, has to take into account space and weather as limiting factors. The farm hand, who generally works without a roof over his head and without a superior at close quarters, operates with a measure of freedom of decision that is most unusual in the case of the industrial worker of corresponding grade. The larger the farm, the greater the need to delegate decisions to the individual; yet under Communist conditions the tendency is generally to do the opposite. Finally, in agriculture—unlike industry— the producer, besides being a consumer of his own product, is mostly also a processor of finished foodstuffs. He is therefore able to alter the pattern of production, utilization, and marketing in many ways and thus to evade public controls far more effectively than the industrial producer, who rarely is a consumer of his product.

Thus, in agriculture, far more than in industry, a relationship of mutual trust is needed between the producer and the state. None of these characteristics of the farming industry has been properly taken into account during the last fifty years of Soviet agricultural history nor during the last fifteen years of Chinese Communist agricultural policy. Instead of concerning themselves with the problems of capital-intensive farming in a growing industrial community, Communist regimes continue to waste their time on the outmoded question of the optimum size of farming. As Marxists have done for the last hundred years, they invariably regard small-scale farming as economically backward and the small-scale operator as politically reactionary and hostile toward the industrial working class. Communist agrarian policy thus becomes an attempt not merely to break with the past, but to act against all precedents; it flies in the face of all historical experience. Nothing like this has ever happened in industry under Communism. Here lies the root of the relatively impressive record of industrialization under Communism and its dismal failure in farming. Only in Communist countries which have abandoned the doctrinal concept of the superiority of large-scale farming, i.e., in Yugoslavia and Poland, has agriculture yielded favorable results.

Had the doctrinal errors in the Marxian agrarian concept been recognized in time, Russia's and China's Communist leaders might never have encountered the predicament of first making the peasants and cultivators their tactical allies in the initial stages of the revolution, and then abandoning them in the interests of collectivization, considered the ultimate aim of "socialism" in agriculture. Instead of turning the peasants and cultivators into their deadliest enemies, Marxist revolutionaries might have succeeded in making them their genuine allies, and thus in combining the fruits of a belated bourgeois reform with those of an industrial revolution.

Communist Agrarian Policy as a Model

In spite of their notoriously poor record in farming, the Communist powers are presenting their agricultural policy, directly and through their international organizations, as a model which others might find worth copying. The columns of Communist periodicals have been filled with contributions on the international aspects of the agrarian question ever since this subject was first discussed by the Communist International in 1920. Before World War II, the Comintern devoted a great deal of attention both to the critical analysis of agricultural policies in non-Communist countries and to the uncritical praise of farming performance in the Soviet Union. In the postwar years the Cominform followed similar lines.

Since the Communists have failed to gain political control in industrially advanced countries, their best hope lies in the underdeveloped, agrarian countries. Among these are the only countries that have accepted the philosophy of the dictatorship of the industrial proletariat. With the advent, in the 1950's, of Soviet economic and technical aid, the Communist knowledge of agrarian conditions in developing countries increased greatly. At the same time, there was a growing awareness of the processes by which industrially retarded countries are made ripe for a Communist seizure of power.[15]

To assist in training international cadres for this purpose, the board of editors of the *World Marxist Review* has at times convened conferences at which representatives from developing countries have met with world Communist leaders. In the Indian state of Kerala and in Indonesia, the Communists have demonstrated the possibility of action in countries in which the agrarian question represents an unresolved political issue. At conferences held under the auspices of the *World Marxist Review* in 1960 in Havana and in Bucharest, it was agreed that "radical agrarian reform is indispensable for rapid development of the productive forces and consequently for social and economic progress."[16] How radical the agrarian reform program is to be depends, however, on the local conditions prevailing at the time of the Communist campaign. Whereas the principal doctrinal stand remains unaltered, a good deal of flexibility is permissible, as it has always been, for reasons of political expediency.

In fact, the concessions that Communist parties and underground organizations are prepared to make for the sake of winning over left-wing bourgeois organizations are substantial. At the same time, a good deal of conventional Communist terminology is retained. Thus, conditions of exploitation in rural areas are described as feudal or semifeudal, irrespective of whether elements of feudalism exist or not. The alliance of workers and peasants is taken for granted, although experienced Communists know that rural and urban interests are not necessarily identical and are often in sharp conflict with each other. Outworn platitudes on the leading role of the industrial proletariat, allegedly the most revolutionary class and thus the motive power of national-democratic movements, are repeated *ad nauseam,* even with regard to countries where there is no trace of an industrial working class as an economic or political force with which to reckon in the foreseeable future.

In line with the current over-all Soviet policy of peaceful coexistence, i.e., expansion of Communist rule by all means short of world war, the concept of cooperation with the national bourgeoisie is considered acceptable for reasons of expediency during the period of transition from "feudalism" to "socialism." No doubt is left, however, about the transitory nature of the alliance with the national bourgeoisie, whose aversion to foreign oppression and colonial exploitation provides a suitable basis for the alliance. The rural bourgeoisie is regarded as capable of being neutralized, if not won over to the cause of agrarian reform.

The Chinese Communists, on the other hand, have not been very successful lately in organizing international gatherings that provide a platform for training revolutionary cadres. The failure in 1965, of the Communist-supported coup in Indonesia has been a severe setback for Chinese prestige in Asia. Nevertheless, the Chinese experience in the agrarian field has not gone unobserved in revolutionary circles. The distinction that some revolutionary leaders make between the lower strata of the peasantry, i.e., the agricultural laborers, the poor and middle peasants, and the upper strata of middle peasants and rich peasants follows the Chinese rather than the Russian pattern.[17]

Agrarian reform is closely associated with the Communist demand for national independence, where this has not been achieved, and for economic independence from "neocolonial exploitation," where political independence is a reality. In the interest of Communist participation in the process of national liberation, substantial concessions are regarded as justifiable by Communist leaders, at least in the present phase. The most significant evidence may be found in the readiness to accept expropriation, with compensation, of landed property above a certain ceiling and its distribution, against a certain charge, to landless farm laborers and tenants. These deviations from conventional Communist doctrine are now considered permissible where a more radical program would antagonize "progressive bourgeois forces" and thus weaken Communist influence in political circumstances otherwise favorable. In Iran, the Tudeh Party insists on the abolition of the landlord system and the transfer of landlord property to the peasants, through confiscation without compensation in the case of "feudal" estates and landlords who have acted as "enemies of the people," but with compensation in the case of big landowners upholding the national interest.

No mention is made in current Communist statements of the ultimate aim of collectivization where such a program could upset the precarious alliance with non-Communist political groups. This is, of course, in line with Communist tradition. It was the practice throughout Eastern Europe, as well as in China, where collectivization was explicitly rejected as the ultimate aim as long as the Communist parties were preoccupied with gaining the mass support of the rural population in the early phases of their seizure of power. The delegates to the agrarian conferences in Havana and Bucharest followed this pattern, except for occasional vague references to the formation of voluntary "cooperatives," which only the initiated could recognize as the forerunners of collectives. Where political developments are far enough advanced, however, as in Cuba, the institutional pattern of the future is revealed. It should not be thought, therefore, that Communist views on agrarian matters cannot undergo certain changes within the over-all doctrinal setting.

As Communist influence extended from Indonesia in the East to Cuba in the West, changes were bound to result in the Communist view of the world and the role of developing countries within the Communist pattern of development. At the Twenty-third Congress of the CPSU in 1966, Prime Minister Kosygin, for the first time in the history of Soviet planning, drew attention to the advantages that the Communist system might gain from an international division of labor. These views are bound to leave their mark on the political priorities of economic development. For over forty years of Soviet history, these had been the expropriation, without compensation, of foreign and indigenous capital, the establishment of heavy industry, and the collectivization of agriculture following the redistribution of the land of large landowners. Cooperation with the national bourgeoisie and conditions that are far more backward than those of Russia in 1917 inevitably call for certain corrections in the established doctrine.

Early in 1965, Professor Kuczynski of the Humboldt University in East Berlin, a lifelong Communist with connections in the centers of Communist thought and power, suggested one of the corrections that had become necessary. In Cuba, he had discovered that the most important recent trend was "the creation of a new industry: agriculture." "The emergence of modern agriculture as an industry, highly mechanised and chemicised," he said, "must be taken into account" when Communists "investigate the possibilities, the ways and means, for the best and fastest economic development in the 'new' countries in the interest of their people."[18]

In his analysis of economic development, Kuczynski distinguished between the "textile way," which England, the

United States, Germany, and France had taken; the "iron-and-steel way," the heroic way, which the Soviet Union had taken, sacrificing rapid progress in material well-being for the sake of rapid progress on her revolutionary path; and the "agricultural way," which—in Kuczynski's view—appears to be the most advantageous approach for newly liberated countries such as Cuba, the first Communist country that has chosen this alternative. If the iron-and-steel way was the only correct and logical way for the Soviet Union, "this does not mean that under present radically changed world conditions every new socialist country must take the iron-and-steel way." In fact, "Cuba's way is a pioneer way of the greatest importance, not only for the building of socialism there, but also to show the way for many countries not yet socialist, but up to now only non-capitalist."

Kuczynski has been in political trouble in the past, particularly when he associated himself with the views held in China during the period of the Hundred Flowers. Since then, however, he has retreated to the line officially accepted in the Soviet Union. He is unlikely, therefore, to have deviated from this line when he expounded his opinion on the "agricultural way to industrialization." Judging by the Cuban precedent, this means that there is no change in the official Communist concept according to which land distribution is to be followed by land concentration in collectives. As the recent history of Cuba has shown, alliances with the urban and rural bourgeoisie are of a tactical nature only. The Chinese view is unlikely to differ in this respect, though in densely populated countries like China the communes are bound to be regarded as more suitable than the collectives.

In view of the importance of Communist opinion on the future of backward agrarian countries, as expressed in such journals as the *World Marxist Review* and the *Labour Monthly,* and at international congresses, seminars and training centers, surprisingly little attention has been paid to these views in the Western world. There is every reason to take them seriously, even though the Communist record in agriculture has little to commend it. The strength of the Communist argument in this area lies in the fact that much of the criticism of conditions in developing countries has a solid enough foundation to make acceptable a solution that might otherwise seem unsuitable; nor is the Communist contention that agrarian reform is a prerequisite of industrialization without foundation. The temptation to follow the Communist pattern is, therefore, likely to remain. It can be resisted only where viable alternatives are presented that invalidate the Communist argument.

Non-Communist Agrarian Alternatives

It is not easy to define the role of agriculture in Western industrialized society. Where government does not plan, the function of individual sectors is largely left to the interplay of political, social, and economic forces. Government interference is usually limited to supporting the farmers sufficiently to raise their incomes to levels comparable with those reached in sectors of the community not exposed to the hazards of nature and the limitations of space. Less significant aspects aside, agriculture in Western industrialized society is thus marked by the fact that it is integrated to such an extent that it is called a farming industry. Those concerned with the production of farm produce are not peasants, but farmers. This means that the bulk of the produce of the industry reaches the final consumer after having passed through the hands of processors and traders instead of being consumed or handled primarily by the producers themselves, as is the case under the conditions of peasant farming. The producer thus does not rely on subsistence farming as his source of livelihood, but on the exchange of goods in national or international markets.

Since his customers are primarily sedentary urban workers, the farmer specializes in meeting their requirements, by producing "protective" foods—dairy products, fruits and vegetables, and animal protein foods, such as milk and meat. By comparison, grains—the chief crops of subsistence farming—lose in importance. Since the pattern of production is determined by the physical requirements of the customer and not by those of the supplier, the farmer behaves in a way that is basically no different from that of the nonagricultural producer. He assesses the success or failure of his performance primarily in financial terms and is therefore prepared to transfer his labor and capital from farming to nonagricultural activities if he finds these more rewarding.

This approach to farming as an industry rather than as a way of life was limited, up to the turn of the century, to England, the first industrialized country that subordinated the role of its agriculture to the requirements of the consumer, and to countries that specialized in exporting farm produce on a large scale, such as the United States, Canada, and Australia. In these countries the ratio of land to labor favored the application of capital, largely in the form of farm machinery and equipment. As a result, productivity was high, and great efforts were made to raise it. By comparison, efforts devoted to the increase in yield per unit of land were limited to cases where intensity (high yield per acre) and productivity (high yield per man) coincided. In continental Europe, the bulk of the farm output was concentrated in peasant holdings, although some of them were fully integrated in the nexus of the market, e.g., in Denmark.

A good description of the peasant was once given by the Russian economist Chayanov:

> The first fundamental characteristic of the farm economy, of the peasant, is that it is a family economy. Its whole organization is determined by the size and composition of the peasant family and by the coordination of its consumptive demands with the number of its

working hands. This explains why the concept of profit in a peasant economy differs from that in a capitalist economy and why the capitalist concept of profit cannot be applied to the peasant economy. The capitalist profit is a net profit computed by subtracting all the expenses of production from the total income. The computation of profit in this manner is inapplicable in a peasant economy because in the latter the elements entering expenses of production are expressed in units incomparable to those in a capitalist economy. . . . So long as the requirements of the peasant family are unsatisfied, since the subjective significance of its satisfaction is valued more highly than the burden of labor necessary for such satisfaction, the peasant family will work for a small remuneration that would be definitely unprofitable in a capitalist economy. . . . Having a surplus of labor and being unable to secure all its necessities with the income derived from the annual wage of its members, the peasant family can utilize the surplus of labor in a more intensive cultivation of its land. . . . For the same reason the peasant family often rents land at an exceedingly high price, unprofitable from a purely capitalistic standpoint, and buys land for a price considerably exceeding the capitalized rent. This is done in order to find a use for the surplus labor of the family, which otherwise could not be utilized under conditions of land scarcity.[19]

In some European countries, farmers and peasants have existed side by side for many years. The different approach of the two sectors of the community caused some of the social tensions that led to political extremism and, ultimately, to explosion, as in Germany and Italy. In Western Europe, the number of people engaged in agriculture remained roughly static up to the outbreak of World War II, though their share in the total employment declined. In Eastern Europe, the nonagricultural sectors were not even able to absorb the natural increase in population, and the countries of Eastern Europe thus tended to become increasingly agrarian in character. The tensions from which they suffered were due largely to overpopulation under the existing patterns of production and to the polarization of property and social status that resulted. Since World War II, similar conditions have prevailed in most of the developing countries of Asia and the other nonindustrialized continents of the world.

In the meantime the process of industrialization has made rapid progress in and beyond Western Europe, and—at long last—large parts of Western European peasant farming have been transformed into farming industries that cater to the market rather than to the producer. Insofar as difficulties are still encountered in the integration of the countries of the Common Market, they are a measure of the strength of the residual peasant element in Western Europe's farming industry. With the exception of Japan and Israel, Asian countries are nowhere near the stage where their cultivators can be turned into farmers. Yet, unless the farm population is integrated into the market economy that is one of the characteristics of industrialized society, serious conflicts are bound to arise from the differences in the pace at which the agricultural and nonagricultural sectors develop.

In Asia, as in Europe, there are, of course, considerable differences from country to country. In countries with an abundance of land, a low over-all density of population, and a favorable land-labor ratio, the political, social, and economic pressure is bound to be less than in countries that are overpopulated, short of land, and poorly endowed with mineral resources. In most countries of Southeast Asia there is still a good deal of land open for cultivation. On the other hand, large parts of India and Indonesia are grossly overpopulated under present conditions of production.

In either case, great differences exist within the rural society. In India, at the end of British rule, less than one-tenth of the agricultural population owned holdings of 25 acres or more; those who farmed these holdings cultivated almost two-fifths of the total acreage, produced one-quarter of the total farm output, and supplied one-third of the total marketed product. At the other end of the scale, three-quarters of the agricultural population cultivated another two-fifths of the total acreage in holdings of less than 10 acres, produced one-half the total farm output, and supplied 45 per cent of the total marketed product.[20] Thus, almost half the market supplies of India were derived from small-holders, many of whom were forced to sell at the expense of their own level of consumption so as to meet their obligations toward landlord and state. This condition still applies. While the large owners look at the use of land in commercial terms, the cultivators and tenants of small holdings are mainly engaged in subsistence farming; their contributions to the supply of the market, though substantial *in toto*, consist of small quantities extracted from many individual cultivators in the form of rent and land tax, and not produced with the final consumer of the product in mind. Even where the process of land concentration and polarization of village society has not gone as far as in India, it is in evidence. There is tension in the economic, social, and political spheres in every country of Asia that has not undergone major changes brought about by agrarian reform.

Agrarian reform, as understood in this context, covers two principal operations: the change of conditions of land tenure aimed at creating security of tenure and reducing tenancy rentals, and the distribution of land belonging to owners of large holdings to small farmers and landless laborers. Other aspects of agrarian reform, such as the consolidation of fragmented farms, the reclamation of virgin lands, the provision of credits for farm improvements, advisory services for the farmers, and cooperative marketing facilities for farm products and farm requisites—although important aspects of any all-embracing program—represent ancillary services and should not be mistaken for the original ingredients of the reform itself. They are best applied after the reforms have been carried out and should certainly not be applied in place of the basic reforms. In fact, this is what often happens, however. Those who wish to discredit agrarian reform or to divert attention from its implementation to side issues, frequently—and quite wrongly—present the aftercare as an alternative to the original cure.

Historical Precedents

This is one of the reasons why some reforms have gone astray in the past and why others will do so in the future. Some analysts who have compared the original objectives of agrarian reforms with the results achieved have gone so far as to conclude that all reforms are destined to fail in some important respects. There is no justification for such a static approach to a basically dynamic process. If agrarian reforms have only partially succeeded in the past, this has been due either to errors in the original design or to counteractions taken by those in favor of the *status quo ante*. In these respects the history of agrarian reforms provides some useful pointers—although it is understood, of course, that history never repeats itself.[21] It would indeed be disastrous if historical precedent were copied in circumstances that are bound to be different in vital respects.

British observers have found it difficult at times to engender much sympathy for the concept of agrarian reforms in Asia. This is largely due to the very special historical circumstances under which the agrarian structure was changed in England. The process started very early, at the end of the Middle Ages, when labor rent was commuted into rent in cash, resulting in a change from a barter economy to one determined by monetary considerations. From the sixteenth to the eighteenth century, common lands were taken into private ownership. Extensive sheep farming took account of the supply of labor reduced by the Black Death and provided the raw material for the Flemish textile manufacturers. Later, the enclosures provided the ground on which arable crops were grown for an increasing industrial population. At the same time, these enclosures created the conditions under which landless peasants turned to industrial employment, and the farming sector became increasingly integrated into an industrial and commercial society. Although the change of the agrarian structure was less violent than in other countries, it nevertheless created a state of extreme concentration of property and polarization in the countryside. At the end of the nineteenth century, less than one-half of 1 per cent of the landowners in England and Wales owned nearly three-fifths of all land under crops.[22] Much of the land was farmed by tenants. While tenancy itself was not necessarily an unsatisfactory arrangement, the absence of security of tenure made important amendments of the tenancy legislation necessary.

By comparison with the British experience, the other two classical cases of agrarian reform in Europe were marked by great violence. In both France and Russia, the property of the landlords was expropriated, without compensation, in the course of revolutions, though in France compensation was granted later, during the Restoration. In both instances the property of the church was also expropriated, and in both cases the revolution opened the way to industrialization and the growth of an industrial proletariat, though in France it initially strengthened the urban and rural bourgeoisie rather than the working class. In Russia, the agrarian reforms ranged over more than half a century, from the emancipation of the serfs in 1861—five hundred years after emancipation had taken place in England—to the substitution, after 1906, of private for communal land under Stolypin, and, finally, at the end of World War I, to the distribution to small peasants and landless laborers of large estates, which ten years later were reconstituted in the form of collectives. Whereas the English and French reforms brought about industrialization, the intensification of agriculture, and the democratization of political institutions, the Russian reforms, though furthering the process of industrialization, failed to create democratic institutions, to strengthen the bourgeoisie, or to intensify agriculture. There are, therefore, lessons to be learned from the historical precedents, though no straight adaptation—let alone direct adoption—is possible.

These lessons might be summarized as follows: First, the earlier agrarian reforms are instigated, the smoother the change from agrarian to industrial society is likely to be (England). Conversely, the longer agrarian reforms are delayed, the more violent the forms that the change is likely to take (France and Russia). Secondly, unless a certain measure of compensation is granted to the expropriated landowners, the reform is likely to be followed by a restoration, during which the dispossessed introduce countermeasures that tend not only to provide compensation, but to invalidate much else that formed an integral part of the original reform (France). Thirdly, unless the expropriated land is distributed to smallholders and landless laborers and is left at their disposal, continued state control becomes necessary; this is bound to have a stifling effect on progress in farm production and on the growth of democratic institutions (Soviet Russia). In any event, agrarian reform serves as a precondition of change where agrarian societies are in the process of becoming urban, industrialized societies. It is not, however, a cure for all economic, social, and political ills, and its effectiveness depends on certain subsequent and supplementary measures that are not a part of agrarian reform itself.

Much of the historical record is generally known among those concerned with problems of social change and economic growth. The *Fourth Report on Progress in Land Reform,* issued by the Secretary General of the United Nations during the thirty-ninth session of its Economic and Social Council, simply assumed that "there is now such a widespread acceptance of the view that land tenure arrangements should be deliberately readjusted in order to promote economic and social development that no further pleading of the merits of that view is necessary."[23] While this may be so, it is also true that most countries in Asia are still far from having made the adjustments in their land tenure conditions on which further development depends. Wolf Ladejinsky, who has done more than any other person alive for the cause of land reform in Asia, has observed that "there is no country in Asia, however underdeveloped, which does not know how to write a reform law, or what its implications might be. They have written them, and many have not been carried out—precisely because the political decision-makers understood their implications and their inevitable repercussions."[24] Most of the governments and parliaments in Asia do not sufficiently represent the cultivators and tenants, who do not yet know how to take care of their own interests.

The defects of the agrarian structure and the obstacles they cause to economic development were set out more than fifteen years ago in the first report of the United Nations on this subject[25] and in the proceedings of the first world conference on land tenure held in Madison, Wisconsin.[26] Since then, four reports on Progress in Land Reform[27] have been published by the United Nations, the last report having been presented at the World Land Reform Conference called by the Food and Agriculture Organization of the United Nations in the summer of 1966. A large volume of analytical material and a fairly full account of success or failure in this sphere can thus be drawn upon.

The defects in the agrarian structure of Asian countries need not be recapitulated here, except to say that the prevailing conditions of land ownership and tenure are repeatedly described in the publications of the United Nations as presenting powerful obstacles to economic development in general and to progress in agriculture in particular. The fatalism that is often found in Asia is attributed to the existing social structure, which in turn is seen largely as the consequence of a particular pattern of land ownership and tenure. As changes in the institutional and industrial pattern take place, reforms of the agrarian structure are regarded as imperative. The legislative measures taken in most, though not all, countries of Asia tend to aim at transferring the ownership of land to the cultivators and at improving the conditions of tenure where tenancy continues to exist. The creation of owner-occupiers is considered a prerequisite for improved cultivation and increased investment in farming, and the change in tenure conditions is expected to lead to a rise in living standards. At the same time, it is recognized that agrarian reforms cannot correct the disparity between land and population where the density of the farm population is high and is on the increase.

The economic, social, and political objectives of agrarian reform are clearly so closely intertwined that it is practically impossible to separate them, but there is a growing trend in national and international publications to give priority to the economic objectives of the reforms that are directed at the allocation of resources and the resulting increase in production and productivity. These are the aspects that are stressed, particularly by those who look with distaste at the social aspects of agrarian reform, such as the redistribution of property, income, and status, that result in a certain degree of social equality. The critics of agrarian reform are generally not impressed by its political aspects either, such as the possible removal of certain causes of tension and the promotion of conditions of political stability.

Effective Agrarian Reforms in the Far East

If the agrarian reforms that have been instigated in Asia since the end of World War II are measured against the objectives that have been set by international agencies, it must be admitted that most of them have fallen short of these targets. The only reforms that can claim to have broadly achieved what they set out to do are those carried out in Japan and Taiwan. These were set in motion soon after World War II, and they have thus had more time to take effect than any of the reforms introduced elsewhere in Asia. More importantly, both in Japan and Taiwan, the American preference for social equality and political stability was able to exert itself to a much greater extent than elsewhere in Asia. While it would be wrong to suggest that the reforms were forced by the victors upon the vanquished, it is probably true that without the vigor and determination of the American occupation forces Japan's reform might have taken on a very different character. Most important of all, however, the power of the landowning classes had been weakened during and after World War II to such an extent that the mobility of landed property, and, with it, that of agricultural labor became possible for the first time. This has not yet happened elsewhere to anything like the same extent, and this is one of the chief reasons for the stagnation of the farming industry in large parts of Asia.

As Ladejinsky, who was one of General MacArthur's advisers, put it, the American role was that of midwife to a reform that had been in its prenatal stage.[28] In Taiwan, the defeat which the Kuomintang (KMT) had suffered on the mainland of China furthered the understanding of the interrelation between agrarian reform on the one hand and economic growth, social equality, and political stability on the other. In Taiwan, the close cooperation between Chinese and American specialists in the Joint Commission for Rural Reconstruction corresponded to the role of "midwifery" played by General MacArthur and his staff in Japan.

The preamble to the law in which the principal provisions of the Japanese agrarian reform were incorporated gave as its purpose the assurance of the right of the cultivators to the fruit of their labor, thereby contributing to the increase of the productive capacity of agriculture and to the promotion of democratic tendencies in the rural communities. The objectives were thus clearly political, social, and economic, and no attempt was made to give one priority over the others. The provisions of the reform, as amended in consultations between the occupation authorities and the postwar government of Japan, were clearly aimed at these objectives, and any loopholes in the legislation were closed as soon as they were discovered. As a result, the implementation of the reform was speedy and decisive, without any of the signs of hesitation that have marked postwar agrarian reforms in other countries of Asia.

Japan had instituted its first agrarian reform during the time of the Meiji Restoration, when the old feudal regime was abolished, title deeds issued, and the alienation of land permitted. These measures brought considerable advantages to the farming community, but on the whole they made the rich richer and the poor poorer than they had been before. To rectify this situation, the postwar reform virtually eliminated absentee ownership, limited the ownership of resident landowners to a permitted ceiling of 3 chō (equal to 3 hectares, or 7.5 acres), fixed the legal maximum of tenant holdings at 1 chō (1 hectare, or 2.5 acres), and turned a large number of tenant farmers into owner-occupiers. While it was not intended to do away with tenancy as an institution, the fixed maximum ceiling of ownership, the secure tenancy conditions, the low purchase prices of land, the speed of the operation, and the existence of a powerful enforcement organization all contributed to the virtual disappearance of farm tenancy. The remaining tenants were given written agreements containing precise terms, including a maximum cash rent equal to 25 per cent of the gross product as standard rental.

The first laws on land reform were enacted almost immediately after the end of hostilities, but they had to be strengthened before they became effective. Thereafter, the reform was implemented within three years, and it was completed by the end of 1950. The ceiling for leased land was fixed, on the average, at 1 chô, except on Hokkaido, where it was 4 chô. The price for land taken over by the state for purposes of redistribution was fixed, well below market value, at the capitalized value of the average net farm return. Purchase and sales prices were the same. Compensation to expropriated landowners was paid in unredeemable land bonds, issued in units of 1,000 yen, which were repayable in equal installments over twenty-five years at 3.6 per cent interest. In fact, owing to a steep inflation, they were repaid within a few years, which amounted to a virtual expropriation, without compensation, of the former landowners. Farmers who had purchased land were expected to pay for it in annual installments over twenty-five years at 3 per cent interest, but the inflation made it possible for them to liquidate their debts very much faster than this.

As a result of the reform, almost 2 million landowners had to part with approximately 2 million hectares (5 million acres), equal to one-third of the total agricultural area. Almost 4.5 million farming families, or 70 per cent of all farm households, benefited from the redistribution of the expropriated land. The operation was in the hands of almost 10,000 locally elected land commissions, each of which consisted of five tenants, three landowners, and two owner-cultivators. All transactions were recorded in the local land register.

The reform was intended to give smallholders and tenants an advantage over the former landowners. In this it succeeded. Japan became a country of owner-occupiers, the first in Asia. Tenancy declined sharply, and, where it remained in force, it was made secure. The acreage of tenanted land declined from 2.4 million hectares (6 million acres), or 46 per cent of the total area farmed, in 1945, to half a million hectares (1.25 million acres), or 10 per cent of the total farm land, in 1950; in the meantime, it has declined further to one-quarter of a million hectares, or 5 per cent of the farmed area. Conversely, the area farmed by owner-occupiers increased from 54 per cent of the total area in 1945 to 95 per cent twenty years later. The change in the status of farm households was correspondingly drastic. The share of owner-occupiers increased from less than one-third of all households in 1945 to four-fifths in 1965, and the share of those who rented more than they owned declined during this period from almost 50 per cent to 5 per cent. During these two decades the average size of farms remained almost unchanged, i.e., slightly less than 1 hectare (2.5 acres) per household, but the deviation from the average became somewhat less marked than it had been before the reform.

As a result of the reform, or simultaneously with it, the rate of economic growth increased and the rate of social inequality declined. Growth rates of gross national product, investment, and personal consumption are now the highest in Asia and among the highest in the world. The productivity of land, labor, and capital in Japanese agriculture increased considerably, as did the input of farm requisites, such as power-driven machines and commercial fertilizers. Agricultural incomes increased as the burden of rent disappeared. At the same time, the organs of local government were greatly strengthened in the rural areas, and the forces of political extremism were weakened. Although the former landowners still have the cards stacked in their favor, feudal relations were mortally wounded by the agrarian reform. One-half the members of the original agricultural committee charged with the implementation of the reform were tenants, who tasted the sweetness of power in the village community for the first time. The experience is unlikely ever to be lost on them. The distinction between the landlord's and the tenant's way of life has been blurred, if not extinguished; and the pattern of expenditure and consumption in the villages is now little different from that of the urban areas, though disposable incomes in rural communities amount to only three-quarters of those in towns.

The Japanese agrarian reform suffered, however, from two serious weaknesses. The number of farmers detrimentally affected was unduly large and the rate of compensation was unduly small. Two million farmers in opposition represent a formidable political problem, all the more so as the payment of compensation in depreciated currency amounted almost to the confiscation of their property. Both factors have caused the reformers a good deal of trouble that might have been avoided. As it was, a certain amount of evasion of the law was inevitable, and it would have occurred on a larger scale, had it not been for the watchful eyes of the American authorities of occupation. There is now some pressure to reopen the question of compensation, as well as a growing demand for an enlargement of the size of farms; however, only part of this is due to economic considerations. If these pressures can be directed toward insufficiently utilized pastures in the hilly parts of the country, no harm need come to those who have benefited from the agrarian reform.

Taiwan, where the two principal errors of the Japanese reform were avoided, fared even better than its neighbor.[29] First of all, the number of landowners who were obliged to sell some of their land was limited to approximately 100,000, or one farm household in seven—a politically more manageable proportion than in Japan; secondly, compensation was arranged so as not to be affected by any deterioration in the value of the currency. The Japanese experience was studied with profit by those concerned with the reform in Taiwan.

The concept of equalization of land rights had been enshrined, as early as in 1905, in the platform of Sun Yat-sen, the political father of modern China. He formulated his views on China's agrarian question at the time when

Stolypin introduced his reform measures in Tsarist Russia. Twenty years later Sun Yat-sen put forward his policy of "Land to the Tillers" as the solution to China's agrarian problems; but it could not be carried out effectively, while the government was preoccupied with warlordism and the Japanese invasion. Thus, the mainland was lost to the Communists, and the KMT had to retreat to Taiwan. At that time, the conditions of landownership and tenure were similar to those of prewar Japan. Nearly two-fifths of all farmers had no land of their own and another quarter were part owners, part tenants. Over half the country's farm area was cultivated by tenants. Although most farms were small, a good deal of property was concentrated in a few hands. Rents were high even by Asian standards, ranging from 50 to 70 per cent of the main crop. In addition, tenants often had to render personal services to the owners whose land they had leased. Leases were mostly verbal and provided no security of tenure.

The postwar agrarian reform was carried out in three phases. First, the Farm Rent Reduction Act brought order into tenure conditions; thereafter, regulations governing the transfer of government-owned land to private owners were issued; and, finally, the Land to the Tiller Act of 1953 laid the foundation for the purchase of land from nonfarming landowners and for its distribution to smallholders and tenants. The ceiling on rent was fixed at 37.5 per cent of the gross return of the main crop. This share was calculated on the assumption that the cost of production equaled an average of 25 per cent of the total crop. On this basis, the remainder was distributed evenly between owner and tenant. Written lease agreements were to cover a minimum period of six years, and expired contracts were subject to renewal. Landowners were entitled to evict tenants only after they had failed to pay their rent for two years or if they sublet the tenanted land. Landowners were obliged to waive rents partially or totally in case of crop damage due to natural disaster. These regulations provided improved living and working conditions for more than half the farm population.

Since the state owned approximately one-fifth of the cultivated area of the country, it was possible to make available to smallholders and tenants some 100,000 hectares (250,000 acres) of public lands. These could be purchased in lots ranging from 0.5 hectare (1.25 acre) of high-quality land to four times as much in case of poor-quality land. The purchase price was fixed at two-and-a-half times the expected average crop, payable in twenty equal semiannual installments. This meant an annual payment equal to the rental of 25 per cent over the period of a decade. The transfer of land was not permitted before the end of this time, and at the end of it the tenants became owners.

The Land to the Tiller Act followed the same pattern, but it contained the additional provision that above a fixed ceiling land became subject to compulsory purchase. This ceiling ranged from 3 hectares (7.5 acres) of paddy land to twice as much in the case of dry land. Payment arrangements for those who purchased any land were identical with those in force for public lands. The former landowners were compensated. They received 70 per cent of the purchase price in commodity bonds and 30 per cent in stocks of government-owned corporations. The cement and paper and pulp corporations absorbed over two-thirds of all government shares; the remaining shares were distributed between the industrial and mining and the agricultural and forestry corporations. The interests of the former landowners were thus directed primarily into nonagricultural channels.

As a result of these reforms, the number of landowners was doubled and that of tenants halved. The share of owners increased from approximately one-third of all farm households in 1949 to two-thirds in 1961. Conversely, the share of tenants declined during this period from two-fifths to one-seventh of all farm households. The area under tenancy declined from over half of the total cultivated area to one-tenth, and that farmed by owner-occupiers increased from less than half to almost 90 per cent. At the same time, credits for long-term investment became available at interest rates of 12 to 15 per cent per annum as against former rates of 36 to 48 per cent on loans that were mostly short-term. The average size of farms declined slightly, from 1.3 hectares before the reform to 1.1 hectares thereafter, but the number of farms of less than 1 hectare increased from one-quarter to one-third. In the meantime, the high rate of population has created growing pressure on Taiwan's limited land resources. This pressure is so great that only part of it can be effectively diverted into nonagricultural activities. Thus, in Taiwan, as in Japan, the agrarian reform has been unable to solve the problem of an unfavorable land-labor ratio; nor was it meant to do so.

Some of the population pressure has been met, however, by growing output. Over-all farm production increased during the ten years after 1952 by over 50 per cent and livestock production, which is still small, more than doubled. The double-cropping index of arable crops increased by about one-tenth; most land in Taiwan is now double-cropped. The input of farm requisites increased by one-fifth, but working capital almost doubled; at the same time, the growth of fixed capital was kept within strict bounds. Labor productivity increased by one-half and land productivity by one-third, while capital productivity declined by one-tenth. The farming industry has thus husbanded its resources well, increased its intensity, and improved its productivity. The expenditure pattern has changed markedly. In 1963, foodstuffs accounted for less than three-fifths of total expenditure, against more than two-thirds in 1948—a clear sign of increased diversification of consumption. The amount of money spent on social and religious occasions doubled during this period.

Some former landowners are reported to have complained about the low efficiency of the public corporations whose bonds they hold; but this seems a relatively minor shortcoming in an otherwise remarkably successful operation. Since some 40 per cent of total compensation has found its way into nonagricultural investment, this novel way of dealing with displaced agricultural capital seems to have met with more favorable response than was originally expected.[30]

Pending Agrarian Reforms on the Indian Subcontinent

The experience of Japan and Taiwan indicates the direction in which agrarian reforms might suitably move elsewhere in Asia. This applies in varying degrees to different countries. However, nowhere else are such essential ingredients as speed, clarity, and simplicity of reform measures and effective enforcement agencies as yet discernible. In Southeast Asia, where population pressure is not unduly great, agrarian reforms may be thought to be less urgent than on the Indian subcontinent; but even in Burma, Ceylon, and Malaysia, and more so in Indonesia and the Philippines, there are areas in which the need for reform of landownership and tenure cannot be denied. The notion that the need for reform is less urgent in South and Southeast Asia today than it was fifteen years ago in Japan and Taiwan is unwarranted. This applies more than anywhere else to the Indian subcontinent, where the fate of Asia may ultimately be decided.

In India, the complexity of the agrarian question almost defies description. A great variety of tenure conditions exist throughout the subcontinent, which is beset by many controversial issues. Apart from the question of land ownership, there are also problems of race, religion, caste, language, and economic growth. It is not altogether surprising, therefore, that progress has been slow, if not disappointing. Even if the interests of the large landowners had not been well entrenched in the party in power, the country might have been denied progress in this sphere. The fate of agrarian reform was sealed once it was decided to leave matters of land ownership and tenure to the state governments. The central government limited itself to making suggestions, issuing guidelines, and publishing progress reports. When independence was granted, central authority was strictly limited. The delegation of power to the states must thus have seemed the obvious solution. Yet, while the central government reserved the right to decide on all major questions of economic growth, social status, and political stability, it abdicated its authority when it surrendered the handling of the all-important land question to the regional authorities.

After independence, the termination of the zamindari system was given highest priority in the agrarian sphere. Since this system was a legacy of British colonial rule, its elimination was a popular measure to which no dissenting voices were likely to be heard. The zamindar had been created as an intermediary who, under conditions of indirect rule, was given the title to collect taxes, provided he paid the colonial administration an annual amount, fixed either in "permanent settlement" or, subject to review every thirty to forty years, under temporary settlement. In turn, the zamindar received title to the revenue-bearing land. The right of tax collection was thus converted into the right of ownership.

While the tax system was fairly lenient when it was created, in time it caused the evil conditions of subtenancies and exorbitant rent collections, which eventually applied to two-thirds of the cultivated area of British India. This form of tenure was most prevalent in Bengal, Bihar, Orissa, and Assam, and in parts of Uttar Pradesh, Madhya Pradesh, and Madras. In the course of time, in these areas land was let through intermediaries either to "occupancy tenants" or to tenants-at-will. Whereas the position of the former was

reasonably secure, the tenants-at-will were in no way protected by law. This situation was described as detrimental to
farm efficiency in the report of the Flood Commission
(1940) and in the report of the Famine Enquiry Commission
(1945). Both reports recommended the abolition of the
zamindari system.

Whereas two-thirds of the cultivated area of British India
thus became the immediate target of postwar legislation, the
remainder continued to be farmed under the ryotwari
system, which also had its institutional weaknesses.* Under
this system the cultivator originally owned his land, but, as
the density of the farm population and the demand for land
increased, so ryotwari land became concentrated in the hands
of a small number of owners, and cultivators were converted
into tenants. By the end of British rule in India, one-third of
the land farmed under the ryotwari system was cultivated in
this way. Thus, it would appear that about three-quarters of
the agricultural area of British India was farmed by tenants.

In 1947, an agrarian reform committee, set up by the
Congress Party, began to review the existing conditions of
land tenure and to formulate a land policy. The chief
recommendation of the committee's report, issued in 1949,
was the abolition of the zamindari holdings and the elimination of all intermediaries between the government and the
cultivator. Expropriated land was to be given to those who
were cultivating it, thus establishing the ryotwari tenure
system in which the cultivator paid taxes directly to the state
and thus became a tenant of the state. Compensation was to
be paid to the former landowners.

At the time of the last prewar census, it was estimated that
less than 5 per cent of the agricultural population were
receivers of rent on an area which accounted for well over

*More recent statistics suggest that, within the present-day boundaries of
India, in 1947 two-fifths of the farm area came under the zamindari system and
three-fifths under the ryotwari system.

half the farming area of British India. The landowners were usually entitled to a rent equal to approximately half the gross product of the land leased, without being obliged to undertake any investment in the improvement of the land. Sometimes they provided working capital in the form of seeds and draft animals. Thus, the tenant not only had to part with half his crop; he also had to bear most of the expenses of cultivating the land, while enjoying little or no security of tenure.

The legislation instigated by the Congress Party after World War II was principally directed at eliminating some of the worst features of the existing system of tenure. Some 20 million tenants were brought into direct relationship with the state. Yet the results of this change fell short of original intentions and expectations. The question of payment of compensation was allowed to delay the enactment of appropriate legislation. Landlords were allowed to contest the constitutional validity of the reform laws, and tenants, being obliged to pay their previous rents in full to the state, were unable to obtain the funds necessary for the acquisition of ownership rights and thus to become owner-occupiers. The decision to treat existing rents as reasonable and to reject as unnecessary an all-round reduction of rents presented a major obstacle to the success of the reform.

In the First Five-Year Plan, the future of land ownership and cultivation was thought to constitute "perhaps the most fundamental issue in national development," and the pattern of economic and social organization was said to "depend upon the manner in which the land problem is resolved." In the Second Five-Year Plan, land reform measures were listed as being of special significance in furthering the cause of economic development and social justice. The objectives of land reform were stated to be: (a) to remove obstacles to agricultural production due to the existing agrarian structure; and (b) to create conditions for developing an agrarian economy with high levels of efficiency and productivity.

Finally, in the Third Five-Year Plan, clause (b), above, was altered to read as follows: to eliminate all elements of exploitation and social injustice within the agrarian system, to provide security for the tillers of soil and assure equality of status and opportunity to all sections of the rural population.

The principal measures to this end were: (1) abolition of intermediaries; (2) reform of tenancy, including regulation and reduction of rent and security of tenure; and (3) conferment of right of ownership on tenants.

There was thus no lack of good intentions at the center of power, but much was left undone in the execution of this policy.[31]

In the absence of central directives and executive powers, considerable differences were allowed to develop between the provisions as laid down by the legislators of individual states. Many of the variations could hardly be justified on grounds of regional peculiarities.[32] Rates of rent were recommended not to exceed one-fifth to one-quarter of the tenant's gross product. In fact, they were fixed at one-quarter to one-half in Kerala, one-third in the Punjab, one-third to two-fifths in Madras, and one-half in Bengal. Even these high rents were effective only where tenants enjoyed security of tenure, which was, in fact, frequently not the case. The regulations providing for the resumption of land by landowners for *bona fide* personal cultivation often led to "voluntary surrenders." Numerous ejections of tenants occurred under the guise of voluntary surrenders, and as a result considerable areas previously held by tenants are now cultivated by laborers. The report of the Planning Commission mentions Hyderabad and Bombay state in particular in this context. The growth of political unrest in these areas was not entirely unrelated to these developments.

Considerable regional differences were also allowed with regard to purchase prices, ceilings of holdings, and compensation of landowners. According to existing land legislation, purchase prices range from fifteen to twenty times the land revenue, or from ten to sixteen times the customary rent. In some cases they are related to the market price, which is usually exceptionally high, owing to the scarcity of land; e.g., in the Punjab the purchase price is fixed at 75 per cent of the market price. Tenants have to pay the price for any land acquired in annual installments ranging over a period of from five to twenty years. The ceiling set on the size of holdings was supposed to be fixed at three times the average family holding, as defined in terms of plow units or work units of a family of average size. In fact, ceilings fixed by state legislation range from 15 to 50 acres, or 25 to 40 "standard acres" (equal to as much as 100 acres of land). According to the report of the Planning Commission, *mala fide* transfers of land have taken place on a considerable scale, with the intention of circumventing the ceilings set on landholdings.

The original proposals of the agrarian reform committee of the Congress Party provided for compensation to be paid to landowners for any land transferred to new owners, but no guidance was given on the expected level of compensation. According to state legislation, the assessment of compensation ranges from twelve to four hundred times the land revenue, or from nine to twelve times the "fair rent," or from three to five times the gross income, or from two to twenty times the net income, or from 25 to 100 per cent of the market value. The bewildering variety of approaches which has resulted from the delegation of power to the states makes interregional comparisons virtually impossible. Whereas much thought has been given to compensation for any losses incurred by former landowners, there seems to be no provision for compensating ejected tenants for any investment made by them in the holdings previously cultivated. Few tenants have become owners of the land they used to cultivate, and few improvements have taken place in the working conditions of farm laborers, of whom there are many millions in India.

It can thus be said, without any reflection on the need for special treatment of regional problems, that major faults have been allowed to develop in the execution of the Indian agrarian reform. It is therefore not surprising that—following the initial success due to the abolition of the intermediaries—the Indian government has not succeeded in satisfying the village population. In the outcome, India has been denied the beneficial effects that followed the postwar agrarian reforms in Japan and Taiwan. While the crop failures of recent years were largely due to unfavorable weather, the apathy of the village population in the face of adverse conditions may fairly be attributed to their disappointment with the execution of the agrarian reform measures. In Ladejinsky's words, "such developments do not produce the incentives which lead to better living conditions, investments in land, improvement of land and a rise in agricultural productivity."[33]

The situation is also unsatisfactory in the non-Indian parts of the subcontinent. In East Bengal (East Pakistan), where the zamindari system prevailed at the end of British rule, the abolition of intermediaries—through the East Bengal State Acquisition and Tenancy Act of 1950—had a salutary effect resembling that in India; but the mere transfer of tenancies to the state did not do away with the harsh conditions under which the tenants operated. The conversion of tenants to owner-occupiers has not yet taken place.

In West Pakistan, the concentration of land and the polarization of village society is particularly marked. Whereas the average size of farm holdings is less than 2 hectares (5 acres), according to data compiled by the Planning Board, before land reform was introduced, some 6,000 persons who were in possession of 200 hectares (500 acres) or more owned half the farm acreage of the country, the other half

being shared by well over 3 million individuals who owned
less than 2 hectares (5 acres) each. This meant that at the top
of the agricultural community the average size of property
was 500 hectares (1,250 acres), but it was less than 1 hectare
(2.5 acres) at the other end of the scale. Half the land was
cultivated by occupier-tenants or tenants-at-will, under conditions similar to those prevailing in India. The case for a
moderate degree of equalization was thus overwhelming. Yet,
the ceiling set on landed property, after ten years of
hesitation and uncertainty, was 200 hectares (500 acres) of
irrigated land or 400 hectares (1,000 acres) of unirrigated
land. In this way, the number of landowners affected by the
reform was kept commendably small; but so was the acreage
of land available for distribution among smallholders, tenants, and landless laborers. Even if all the agricultural land of
West Pakistan had been available for equitable distribution,
this would have provided no more than 2 hectares (5 acres)
per family. As the reform was designed, it left most of the
cultivators with less than the basis of subsistence farming,
without providing for alternative sources of employment or
income.

Soon after independence, an agrarian reform committee
was set up.[34] Its report included the following recommenda-
tions: (a) immediate abolition and cessation of free grants of
land, without compensation; (b) extinction of occupancy
rights in land and conferment of property rights on occupancy tenants; (c) prohibition and abolition of feudal
servitudes and illegal dues and exactions from the tenants; (d)
provision of adequate security of tenure to the tenants-at-
will; and (e) provision of substantial and adequate shares for
the actual tillers in the produce of the soil.

The position remained under examination, and, although a
Land Reform Scheme and a Tenancy Bill were prepared, the
provincial government took no action designed to pass
legislation or to implement the reform in any other way.
When Mohammed Ayub Khan seized power in Pakistan, in

October, 1958, he declared from his post as Martial Law Administrator that land reforms would be carried out "in a scientific manner," since there was a direct relationship between land reform, economic development, and social growth. A land reform commission was appointed to recommend measures for ensuring improved production, social justice, and security of tenure for those engaged in farming. Its report, submitted in January, 1959, recorded the following features as among the chief weaknesses of the existing system of land ownership and tenure:

(1) congestion of land, yet slow development of large estates in spite of pressure of population, resulting in uneconomic and fragmented units of cultivation, evidence of unused land capable of cultivation;

(2) limited access to opportunities, resources of land and manpower not being fully utilized, absence of initiative and enterprise, lack of security of tenure for those engaged in production, absence of reward proportionate to effort and hence of incentive for improved production, lack of encouragement for capital formation and productive investment in agriculture;

(3) concentration of power in the hands of a privileged few, hampering the free exercise of political rights and stifling the growth of democratic institutions.

The commission's minimum program of agrarian reform contained the following measures:

(1) ceiling on individual ownership, so as to break the concentration of landed property, to narrow down inequalities of opportunity, and to encourage the intensive use of land and productive investment;

(2) acquisition of land in excess of the ceiling for redistribution to landless tenants and holders of uneconomic holdings on payment of a fair price;

(3) conversion of occupancy tenancies into full owner-
    ship;

(4) abolition of jagirs (free grants of land or assignments
    of land revenue) and elimination of any form of
    intermediaries, so as to simplify the tenure system
    and to relieve the crowding of interests in land;

(5) security of tenure to tenants, provision of a fair
    fixed rent, elimination of illegal exactions, compen-
    sation for improvements in case of premature distur-
    bance, so as to provide the incentive for a fair return
    proportionate to effort;

(6) encouragement of a strong middle class; laying the
    foundation for owner-operated farms on holdings of
    economic size through consolidation of holdings and
    prevention of fragmentation of holdings;

(7) expansion of cooperatives; and

(8) improvement of the conditions of employment of
    agricultural workers.

Within a week after the commission's report had been
issued, Ayub Khan, as President of Pakistan, announced his
program for the rectification of defects in the agrarian
structure due to absentee landlordism, concentration of
landed wealth, and the fragmentation of land. All the
measures recommended by the commission were incorporated in this program, which was given effect in the West
Pakistan Land Reforms Regulations of February, 1959, when
it became part of the constitution. All regulations were
formulated in a commendably clear form. Compensation of
former landowners was fixed on a progressively diminishing
scale for progressively increasing sizes of property, at an
average of ten times the rental value. This was calculated in
terms of produce index units which took into account
differences in the productivity of the land. Payment of
compensation was made through bonds which were trans-
ferable but not negotiable, and which carried an annual

interest rate of 4 per cent. The bonds were redeemable within twenty-five years.

As carried out in West Pakistan, the reform had a number of encouraging features. At the same time, it suffered from some serious weaknesses. Whereas the compensation of landowners was fixed at 5 rupees or less per produce index unit, the price at which the land became available was pitched high, i.e., at 8 rupees per unit. Moreover, the alienation of land by landowners affected by the reform was permitted, provided that it occurred before April, 1960, or more than a year after the land reform regulations had been promulgated. This provision further reduced the area available for redistribution below its original, modest level, due to the generous maximum ceiling of landholdings. As a result, less than 5 per cent of the cultivated area of West Pakistan became available for redistribution. This was equal to half an acre for each of the persons farming less than 5 acres. Thus the reform, though well designed, had a favorable effect only on a small number of cultivators. A less liberal ceiling would have led to results closer to the spirit of the reform.

Agrarian Reform Measures in Other Parts of Asia and the Far East

Space does not permit a country-by-country coverage of landownership and tenure conditions in Asia and the Far East, or of measures aimed at eliminating any anomalies that exist. However, it may be said without any exaggeration that concentration of landed property and polarization of the rural community, with the familiar characteristics that accompany these phenomena, can be found in all the countries of the area, particularly where land or water, or both, are scarce. Where dry land is plentiful, as in some parts of Ceylon and Burma, unsatisfactory tenure conditions are largely limited to the paddy lands. Where commercial crops are grown in plantations, as in Ceylon, Malaya, and Indonesia, the problems of the plantation workers are quite different from those of the small owner-occupiers, though their lack of security often compares with that of the tenants-at-will. They are frequently of alien descent (e.g., Indian Tamils) and thus sometimes subject to racial or religious discrimination.

Most countries in the area have introduced reforms of one kind or another, but many of these measures have been ineffective, if not actually harmful. Ample evidence to this effect was contained in the reports that were submitted by national delegations to the World Land Reform Conference held in 1966 at the headquarters of the Food and Agriculture Organization of the United Nations in Rome. Public concern is beginning to replace previous instances of self-congratulation. Only a decade or so ago, the questionnaire of the United Nations on progress in land reform was answered by some in a rather casual manner. The Government of Malaya stated on that occasion that conditions among Malays, who are Muslims, had not favored the growth of a landlord class; yet, the "Padi Cultivators (Control of Rent and Security of Tenure) Ordinance" had just been issued "to meet conditions in districts in which landlordism was prevalent."[35] Legislation regulating the conditions of ownership and tenure on paddy lands has also been promulgated in Ceylon and Thailand.

The report submitted by the Thai delegation to the World Land Reform Conference of 1966 stated that rent control was introduced for the first time in 1951, when rents were fixed in relation to yields, but that this measure was not considered very effective, as "the law was ignored even by the tenants themselves, as well as by the Government authorities."[36] In Ceylon, the present government felt that the Paddy Lands Act of 1953 had not gone far enough to bring about a change in relations between landlords and tenants. The Paddy Lands Act of 1958 was intended to improve matters; yet, the report submitted by the Ceylonese delegation to the Conference observed that the tenant cultivators themselves were either indifferent or not well enough organized to press the government for the effective implementation of the Act. As a rule, the traditional half-share of the produce is still being paid to the landlord, and payment of the rent stipulated in the Paddy Lands Act is the exception rather than the rule.[37] In the Philippines, the Agricultural Land Reform Code, passed and approved in 1963, abolished share tenancy and declared it contrary to public policy; yet until recently, share tenants did not approach the landowners unless called. "For the share-tenants to serve notice on their landowners was tantamount to giving them orders"—an unheard of thing.[38]

In most countries of the area, reform measures have only scratched the surface of the problems connected with the existing conditions of landownership and tenure. In several cases, these measures have led—as they did in India—to tenants "voluntarily" surrendering their rights (Nepal) or being evicted (Ceylon). Although some of the errors of the past are being corrected, this is not so in all cases. The political implications of hesitation, neglect, or failure are obvious. Understandably, the resistance of landowners to any encroachment on their rights represents a strong obstacle to reform, and only where government action is speedy, determined, and effective is there a chance of success. In this connection, the reform which is being carried out in Iran is of interest, although the country lies outside the boundaries of the region as defined by the United Nations Economic Commission for Asia and the Far East.

The Iranian Experiment

The need for agrarian reform has been recognized for some

time by most observers of the Iranian scene. The conservative ·landowning aristocracy seemed unlikely to give way to the demands of a rapidly growing urban middle class which represented as its own the demands of the restive elements among the villagers; yet this is what has happened. Before the Shah authorized Ali Amini to rule by decree and referendum, thus making possible a revision of the previous ineffective land reform legislation, less than 5 per cent of the rural population owned nine-tenths of the arable land of the country. A few wealthy families owned half the land and half the villages—most of them lock, stock, and barrel. Religious organizations controlled another quarter, and the Shah himself owned one-tenth of the land. In 1951, the Shah began to distribute some of his land to his tenants. In 1958, part of the public domain was earmarked in a similar way. By 1960, the government had been empowered to acquire any property owned by private individuals in excess of 400 hectares (1,000 acres) of irrigated land or 800 hectares (2,000 acres) of unirrigated land. This was no more than a first, rather timid, beginning; yet the law authorizing the government to carry out the reform was amended by the Majlis (the Iranian parliament) to such an extent as virtually to invalidate the original law.

Early in 1962, the Shah approved a new land reform law, drafted over the signature of the Minister of Agriculture, Nasan Arsanjani, who served under Dr. Amini, himself a landowner of substantial means. The ceiling set under the new law was fixed at one village, a measure more appropriate than the size of the property in a country where land registration was irregular or nonexistent and landowners owned villages rather than farms. At the time of the reform, tenure conditions were normally governed by the principle that land, water, seed, draftpower, and manpower were each worth one-fifth of the gross product. In many instances, the landowners were thus able to claim three-fifths of the crop in return for providing land, water, and seed, although they provided little, if any, capital for farm improvement.

In its first phase, the Iranian land reform was concerned primarily with the acquisition and redistribution of villages owned by landowners in excess of one village. In the second phase, the reform was directed at regulating the relations between landlords and tenants where the latter were unable to become owner-occupiers. The implementation of the reform was placed under the direction of an agrarian reform council and an agrarian reform organization operating under the council. Landlords were offered compensation, calculated as a multiple of taxes paid, in fifteen annual installments, mostly given in the form of bonds issued by the agricultural bank. Cultivators buying the land had to pay the purchase price, plus a charge of 10 per cent, in fifteen equal annual installments. On becoming owners, they were obliged to join an agricultural cooperative society, which was founded to provide services, such as the supply of irrigation water, that were previously the responsibility of the landlord.

The reform was introduced experimentally in the Maragheh area. As the law began to be applied, right- and left-wing opposition to it grew. This was fed, on the right, by large owners and mullahs—who were owners in their own right —and by members of the National Front founded by Mohammed Mossadegh. At the same time, the reform was criticized by the political left which had the support of the National Voice of Iran—broadcasting from Russia—and of Radio Moscow. The argument on the left was that Dr. Amini's government was "administering aspirin and sedatives to someone suffering from cancer" and that "the only remedy was a surgical operation which was beyond the power of Dr. Amini and should therefore be entrusted to a surgeon."[39] The attacks emanating from Russian soil stopped when cordial relations were established between the Soviet Union and Iran. The attacks from the right concen-

trated on denouncing the agrarian reform law as unconstitu-
tional, leaving open the question whether the land subject to
redistribution had been acquired in a constitutional manner
in the first place.

The government eventually gave way to some of the
criticism coming from the right. A number of concessions
were made to the landlords. Owners of whole villages were
given the choice of keeping an aggregate of certain parts of
several villages instead of a single village, and were thus
allowed to gain strategic positions, such as the control of
wells and irrigation waters, in several of the villages they
owned. In this way the effectiveness of the reform was
seriously undermined. There were other weaknesses inherent
in the provisions of the law. The machinery set up for the
enforcement of the law was manned by only a few
insufficiently trained executive officers. Moreover, the purchase price was so high as to be beyond the means of many
cultivators. Finally, such organizations as village councils and
cooperative societies, which were to take over the functions
of the former landowners, were often staffed with inexperienced personnel and were insufficiently endowed with
funds. Considering these weaknesses, the acquisition of
approximately one-fifth of all villages and the distribution of
land to almost half a million families are respectable
achievements. Yet, substantial difficulties remain. The resignation of Dr. Amini in 1962 and the replacement, in 1963, of
his Minister of Agriculture, Dr. Arsanjani, by Lieutenant
General Esmail Riahi led to a reduced pace in the implementation of the land reform legislation. It remains to be seen
whether the Shah will gain no more breathing space than
Stolypin gained fifty years earlier, and whether his reform
measures will achieve what Kerensky failed to achieve before
him. The parallel with the history of agrarian reform in
neighboring Russia can hardly have escaped the Shah and his
ministers. Whatever its outcome, the experiment of a

benevolent monarch in Western Asia deserves as much attention as the reforms carried out on its Eastern offshore islands, Japan and Taiwan.

Summary and Conclusions

Since some of the agrarian reforms in Asia are not well known outside the area, a descriptive, rather than analytical, approach has seemed appropriate here. The view expressly stated in the last of the United Nations progress reports on land reform has been accepted implicitly, i.e., that the conditions of landownership and tenure require readjustments in most cases and that no further pleading of the merits of that view is necessary. Yet, the opposing view has to be taken into account.

Advocatus diaboli will argue, no doubt, that the status quo deserves to be maintained, since landowners are happy to see no change, and smallholders and tenants know no better; that output and yield will decline as the result of any disturbance of existing conditions of tenure; that the new owners will consume more but deliver less than their predecessors; and that in any case the problems of rural overpopulation and underemployment cannot be solved by agrarian reform. Even if all of these arguments were valid, the fact remains that no government in Asia wishes to support such views openly. Arguments of this kind are as old as agrarian reform. They have been put forward wherever effective changes of outmoded agrarian structures have been introduced, as in East Prussia in the 1920's and Japan in the 1950's. Where such reforms have been effective, the village community has become more homogeneous than it was before—in its social composition, its economic interests, and its political affiliations. This does not mean that an egalitarian society has been created or, indeed, intended.

The question may be asked whether there can ever be a

successful program of agrarian reform. The answer to this question depends on what is expected of the reform and what it is supposed to achieve. Elias Tuma, in his comparative analysis, set the targets of agrarian reforms so high as to find all of them wanting—except in the "socialist" countries, i.e., in the Soviet Union.[40] If agrarian reform is seen not as an aim in itself, but as a tool with which to create political stability in place of tension, social equilibrium in place of polarization, and economic growth in place of stagnation, there is enough in the reforms that have taken place in Asia, and in Japan and Taiwan in particular, to justify the view that no further pleading of the merits of the case is required. What is needed in Asian countries that have not yet found a *modus vivendi* adequate to their modern requirements is the will to go ahead with reforms of the agrarian structure which underlies all else—so as to avoid revolutionary explosions that may cause greater damage to the existing political, social, and economic fabric than well-designed reforms are likely to do. In such a situation it is necessary to acquire knowledge of the technical details of existing reforms, without which failures become almost a certainty.

Where agrarian reforms have been carried out with clarity, speed, and determination, supplemented by such ancillary services as credit and marketing cooperatives, and supported by land consolidation, reclamation, and settlement policies, there have been no grounds for looking back with nostalgia at the *status quo ante.* Modern industrialized society requires a type of farm industry that is apt to be handled better by owner-occupiers than by either the owners of large, extensively farmed estates or their tenants. As the owner-occupiers begin to produce the foodstuffs required by industrial workers and other urban dwellers, they contribute toward broadening the domestic market, in which highly qualified "protective" foods are exchanged for the products of the industries producing farm requisites and manufactured consumer goods. In such a situation the economies of scale can look after themselves; they tend, in any case, to be more limited under conditions of intensive farming than in either extensive farming or industry. For a long time to come, industry will at best absorb some part of the net increase of population. Only when both farming and the nonagricultural sectors of society have become capital-intensive will an absolute decline in the numbers engaged in agriculture become feasible. Agrarian reforms can contribute toward laying the groundwork for a more balanced political structure, a more open society, and a more mixed economy than exist at present in most countries of Asia.

Notes

1. L. E. Howard, *Labour in Agriculture* (London, 1935).
2. W. Klatt, "Chinese Agriculture as a Model for Asian Countries," in E. F. Szczepanik (ed.), *Symposium on Economic and Social Problems of the Far East* (Hong Kong, 1961; New York, 1968).,
3. Introduction to W. Klatt (ed.), *The Chinese Model: A Political, Economic and Social Survey* (Hong Kong, 1965; New York, 1965).
4. A. Aziz-W. Klatt, "The Development and Utilization of Labor Resources in South East Asia," in P. W. Thayer (ed.), *Nationalism and Progress in Free Asia* (Baltimore, 1956).
5. W. Klatt, "Labour in Asia," in Guy Wint (ed.), *Asia: A Handbook* (London, 1965; New York, 1966).
6. W. Klatt, "Problems of Development in Asia," in *ibid.*
7. W. Klatt, "Development Aid for Development's Sake," in J. Degras and A. Nove (eds.), *Soviet Planning: Essays in Honour of Naum Jasny* (London and New York, 1964).
8. Naum Jasny, *The Socialized Agriculture of the USSR* (Stanford, 1949).
9. W. Klatt, "Soviet Farm Output and Food Supply in 1970," in *St. Antony's Papers* (Oxford, 1966).
10. W. Klatt, "The Pattern of Communist China's Agricultural Policy," in Klatt (ed.), *The Chinese Model.*
11. K. C. Kao, *Agrarian Policy of the Chinese Communist Party, 1921-1959* (London, 1960).
12. Friedrich Engels, *The Peasant Question in France and Germany* (Moscow, 1955).
13. V. I. Lenin, *Collected Works,* Vol. XXIV (Moscow, 1932).
14. Rosa Luxemburg, *The Russian Revolution* (New York, 1940).
15. V. Bochkaryov, "New Path for New States," *New Times,* No. 41 (October, 1961).
16. W. Klatt, "The Agrarian Question," *Survey,* No. 43 (August, 1962).

17. "The Agrarian Problem and the National-Liberation Movement," *World Marxist Review,* IV, No. 1 (January, 1961).
18. J. Kuczynski, "Modern Agriculture Under Socialism," *Labour Monthly* (London), February, 1965.
19. P. A. Sorokin, C. C. Zimmerman, and C. J. Calpin, *A Systematic Source Book in Rural Sociology* (Minneapolis, 1931).
20. D. Narain, *Distribution of the Marketed Surplus of Agricultural Produce by Size of Holding in India 1950* (New Delhi, 1961).
21. Elias H. Tuma, *Twenty-six Centuries of Agrarian Reform: A Comparative Analysis* (Berkeley, 1965).
22. G. Garbury and T. Bryan, *The Land and the Landless* (London, 1908).
23. United Nations, *Fourth Report on Progress in Land Reform* (New York, 1966).
24. Wolf Ladejinsky, "Agrarian Reform in Asia," *Foreign Affairs,* XLII, No. 3 (April, 1964).
25. United Nations, *Defects in Agrarian Structure* (New York, 1952).
26. Kenneth H. Parsons, *Conference on World Land Tenure* (Madison, Wis., 1951).
27. United Nations, First, Second, Third, and Fourth Reports on *Progress in Land Reform* (New York, 1954, 1956, 1962, and 1966).
28. R. P. Dore, *Land Reform in Japan* (London and New York, 1959).
29. C. Chen, *Land Reform in Taiwan* (Taipei, 1961).
30. Y. T. Chang, "Land Reform and its Impact on Economic and Social Progress in Taiwan," *Industry in Free China,* XXXIII, No. 4 (April, 1965).
31. V. M. Dandekar, *A Review of Land Reform Studies* (New Delhi, 1961).
32. Government of India, *Progress in Land Reform* (New Delhi, 1963).
33. Ladejinsky, *op. cit.*
34. West Pakistan Land Commission, *Implementation of Land Reforms Scheme* (Lahore, 1966).
35. United Nations, Second Report on *Progress in Land Reform* (New York, 1956).
36. World Land Reform Conference, *Country Papers: Thailand* (mimeo.) (Rome, 1966).
37. World Land Reform Conference, *Country Papers: Ceylon* (mimeo.) (Rome, 1966).
38. World Land Reform Conference, *Country Papers: Philippines* (mimeo.) (Rome, 1966).
39. Radio Moscow, February 19, 1962 (in Persian), in *Summary of World Broadcasts* (London, 1966).
40. Tuma, *op. cit.*

Note: Certain sections of this paper have appeared in slightly different form in James R. Brown and Sein Lin (eds.), *Land Reform in Developing Countries* (Hartford, Conn.: The University of Hartford, 1968).

III

THE SOCIAL BASES OF INDIAN COMMUNISM

Donald S. Zagoria

Introduction

Serious students of Communism have done little to elucidate
its social basis. With a few notable exceptions, the writing on
Communism has dealt with historical and political questions.
As a result, the subject has been left to the political
sociologists and to a few theorists whose major concept is
"mass society." The thesis of the latter group is that
uprooted individuals are the ones most likely to support
extremist or totalitarian movements. William Kornhauser, for
example, has argued that extremist mass movements are
likely to develop during periods in which "the most severe
discontinuities in community life occur" and, "as a result,
people are prepared psychologically for all kinds of extremist
behavior they would reject as members of established groups
and social institutions."[1] According to Adam Ulam, Marxism is rooted not in social crises in general but in the
industrialization crisis in particular. He contends that Marx-

The author would like to express his appreciation to the Research Institute on
Communist Affairs, Columbia University, which has supported his research on the
project.

ism "reproduces the social psychology of the period of transition from a pre-industrial to an industrial society."[2] More recently, in a remarkable series of lectures on totalitarian revolutions, Richard Lowenthal has suggested that behind all such revolutions, "we can discover a prolonged 'incubation period' of social and spiritual malaise, due to specific disproportions of development caused by a critical acceleration of uncoordinated social change."[3]

All these theorists thus seem to agree that the appeal of Communism is directly related to rapid, disjointed changes that wrench certain social strata from their traditional roots and values. Communism, seen in this perspective, is the ideology not so much of the worker or peasant as of the uprooted, the individuals of all classes and strata cut adrift from traditional and familiar loyalties and facing new and thorny problems of social adjustment. Indeed, Seymour M. Lipset contends that such "displaced" social groups are always attracted to extremist politics; for him, the real question is which strata are most displaced in each country, since different groups are attracted to different kinds of extremist politics.[4]

The displacement theory undoubtedly helps to explain one of the social sources of Communism, particularly in the underdeveloped areas. But the social sources of Communism are more varied than this theory suggests.

Erik Allardt has pointed out, in an empirical study of Finnish Communism, that in some areas of Finland one could well speak of an "institutionalization of radicalism." In such areas it would be entirely wrong to say that Communist supporters are unattached individuals. On the contrary, they are strongly attached to their communities, but they are, nevertheless, isolated from the national political and social system.[5] Moreover, Allardt distinguishes between two kinds of Communism in Finland, one which he calls "backwoods Communism" and the other "industrial Communism." The former is correlated with rapid economic change, social insecurity, and migrations; the latter, with strong political traditions, stable social conditions, slight economic change, and a comparatively rigid class structure. Comparable distinctions can be discerned in India and elsewhere in the developing countries.

Still another approach to explain the social bases of Communism is to emphasize the susceptibility of certain occupational groups and social strata. Using survey and election data, empirical theorists such as Linz, Hamilton, Kornhauser, and Lipset have found a relationship between working-class radicalism and certain social variables. The typical radical worker is male, nonreligious, of low social status, and a member of a radical union. He most likely lives and/or works in a homogenous community that exposes him to a high degree of intraclass communication; lives and/or works in an isolated community or industry; has little perceived opportunity of upward social mobility; has few if any national crosscutting pressures operating on him; and is a member of a minority group.[6]

What few empirical studies we have of rural radicalism suggest that the peasant most susceptible to radical movements: lives in an area where the old rural elite has been weakened; has had his traditional value system modified by education, literacy, military service, entry into the market, closeness to towns, accessibility to communications, etc.; is a sharecropper, agricultural laborer, or dwarf owner (i.e., under one acre); is found in certain crop areas such as rice and sugar which are labor-intensive, or one-crop areas susceptible to market fluctuations rather than areas with multiple crops.[7]

Yet another explanation of the social bases of Communism in underdeveloped areas is the "communal" theory,[8] which holds that the Communists are able to exploit a considerable variety of ethnic, regional, religious, and other "communal" tensions.[9] But whereas communal alienations of one kind or another have presented the Communists with opportunities in some areas, in others they have been an obstacle. Moreover, there are certain limitations on the ability of the Communists to exploit communal aspirations.

Studies of voting behavior in India, where communalism is a pervasive phenomenon, show that although there is a correlation between voting and community, no communities vote en bloc for one party. The votes of each community are generally split, although this is more true of some communities than of others. In short, although community is an extremely important factor in determining voting behavior and political loyalty, other factors—such as organization, personality, economic class, and ideology—cut across and modify social cleavages. As the authors of one key study of Indian voting behavior assert, the simple view that "politics is only a reflection of the prevailing structure of society, thus making it appear as a mere epiphenomenon," is not tenable.[10]

This chapter will test these theories by examining the social bases of Indian Communism, particularly in Kerala, the one state where it is extremely strong. The following questions will be raised: To what social groups do the Indian Communists direct their appeals and with what success? Do these social groups represent the most displaced groups in society? Do they represent specific communities or classes? If displacement and communalism do not wholly explain Communism's appeal, what other factors enter into it?

Whatever the merits of this particular study, the importance of research on the social bases of Communism in underdeveloped areas seems both undeniable and urgent. In the first place, such research can provide empirical evidence to support or refute the various theories of the appeal of Communism. Second, it is doubtful whether political-strategic questions constantly under review by Communist parties can ever be fully understood without probing into the social base of the particular party. The "left-wing adventurism" of the Chinese Communist Party in recent years is explained by some Marxist theoreticians on the basis of its peasant origins. The struggle between the two wings of the Indian Communist Party today cannot be adequately understood without an appreciation of the trade-union and national base of the moderate, right-wing Communists and the regional and peasant base of the more militant left-wing Communists.[11] Similarly, the factional dispute within the Indian Communist Party during 1948-51 had a great deal to do with the respective social bases of the two factions. It was an anthropologist who pointed out that the Andhra Communists, one of whose bases was the rich peasants of the Kamma caste, were unreceptive to the proletarian, anticapitalist policies of the leader of the Party at that time, B. T. Ranadive, whose base of support lay in the Bombay trade unions.[12] The Andhra group, labeled "kulak pettamdars" (rich landlords) by their Communist adversaries, because they were led by the sons of rich peasants, eagerly seized upon Mao Tse-tung's line of tactical collaboration with the rural rich, since their own social bases dictated extreme caution in pursuing class warfare.

There is not, of course, a simple and direct correlation between the social base of a Communist Party, or any other political party, and its political strategy. The examples cited above suggest that a peasant base can dictate either moderate or militant policies. The point is that much of the past writing on Communism has treated the subject in a social vacuum. To write about the Andhra-Ranadive episode without mentioning its social aspects is surely to miss a crucial part of the problem.

A third reason for stressing the importance of sociological analysis lies in the earlier tendency to stress the uniformities in the Communism of different areas rather than the particularities. This was in part a result of the theory of totalitarianism; in part because most of the pioneering work on Communism was done by specialists on Russia, who tended to look upon Communism in other areas as an extension of Soviet Communism; and in part because local Communist parties imitated Bolshevik models of organization, used Bolshevik jargon, and subscribed to Bolshevik ideology.

For these, and perhaps other, reasons, the particularities of Communism in specific areas and the relationship between Communist parties and their local environments, were left to area specialists who, for the most part, were interested only tangentially in Communism. The result was that local Communist parties were analyzed at one extreme as an integral part of an international movement and at the other as a "normal" political party notable only for its use of a certain ideological jargon.

In recent years, the Sino-Soviet split and the increasingly pluralistic developments within international Communism have stimulated a growing interest in particular Communist parties. Still, there has been little systematic effort to explore the social roots of Communism. For example, there are only one or two biographical studies of a Communist leadership. Only recently has there been a pioneering effort to relate Laotian Communism to the conflict between montagnards and lowlanders and Nepalese Communism to the caste structure in Nepal.[13]

It is with this gap in mind that this study of the social bases of Indian Communism has been undertaken. The bewildering variety of social tensions that pervade Indian politics, and that differ from state to state and region to region, make India a kind of microcosm of the social alienations existing in underdeveloped countries. It is hoped, therefore, that this study will also shed light on Communism's appeal in underdeveloped areas generally.

Two caveats are in order at the outset. First, this is a

preliminary discussion that draws on a larger study now underway, and the conclusions offered here are tentative. Second, it is extremely difficult to obtain reliable data for such a study. To take but one example, Indian census figures since independence have not included caste, except for the Harijans (untouchables). Correlations between caste and voting behavior must therefore be estimated on the basis of earlier census figures, or indirectly worked out. This naturally makes for some margin of error. Despite these limitations, however, it is hoped that the following discussion may offer some insight into the social bases of Communism in India.

Communism in Kerala

The state of Kerala is one of three states in which Communism has a considerable hold on the electorate. As Table I indicates, only in Kerala and West Bengal did the Communists contest more than 50 per cent of the seats in the 1962 elections to the State Legislative Assemblies. In Andhra Pradesh, the third state in which there is substantial Communist influence, the Communists contested a little less than half the total number of seats. Moreover, as Table II shows, Communist strength in Kerala extends throughout the state. In the 1960 elections to the State Legislative Assembly, although the Communists did not regain the power that they lost in 1959, they nevertheless succeeded in winning more than 40 per cent of the vote in six of Kerala's nine districts and more than 30 per cent in two others.

There are four major communities in Kerala. The Christians constitute 24 per cent of the population; the low-caste Ezhavas and Harijans, 34 per cent; the upper-caste Nairs and Brahmans, 19 per cent; and the Muslims, 20 per cent.

Occupation and community in Kerala are to some extent related. A large percentage of the Ezhavas and Harijans are at the very bottom of the economic ladder. They are agricultural laborers, sharecroppers or workers on the large tea, rubber, coir, and cashew-nut plantations. It has been estimated that about 70 per cent of the Nairs are landowners;[14] but most of the landowners in Kerala own very small pieces of land, often less than one acre. As Table III indicates, the extent of dwarf holdings in Kerala runs from four to twelve times the Indian average. Muslims in Kozhikode (Calicut) are engaged in trade and commerce; however, those in Palghat are largely agricultural laborers or fishermen.

TABLE I

NOMINEES FOR STATE ASSEMBLIES, 1962

State	Total Number of Seats	Seats Contested By	
		Congress Party	Communist Party
Andhra Pradesh	300	300	136
Assam	105	103	31
Bihar	318	318	84
Gujarat	154	154	1
Kerala[a]	133	133	78-73
Madhya Pradesh	288	288	43
Madras	206	205	68
Maharashtra	264	264	56
Mysore	208	208	31
Orissa[b]	140	. . .	. . .
Punjab	154	154	47
Rajasthan	176	176	45
Uttar Pradesh	430	429	145
West Bengal	252	252	146

SOURCE: *Report on the Third General Elections in India, 1962,* Vol. II (Statistical), Election Commission, India.

[a]The figures for Kerala are for the 1965 election to the State Legislative Assembly. The first figure is for the right wing of the Communist Party and the second for the left wing.

[b]Orissa did not hold Assembly elections in 1962, and figures for other years were not available.

There is also a correlation between community and region. The Ezhavas are the majority community in Palghat, one of the three districts of Malabar, which, in 1956, was combined with the former princely state of Travancore-Cochin to form the linguistic state of Kerala. Large numbers of Ezhavas are also to be found in the coastal belts of Travancore-Cochin, where the big plantations are located. The Muslims are concentrated in Malabar, particularly in Cannanore and Kozhikode (Calicut), whereas the Christians are concentrated in three or four districts of Cochin and Travancore. The combination of Malabar and Travancore-Cochin to form Kerala made the Ezhavas, numerically dominant in Malabar, the largest single community in the new state.

All of the communities are well organized. The Christians have their churches.[15] The Nairs have the Nair Service Society (NSS) and the Ezhavas have the Shri Narayan Dharma Paripalana Yogam (SNDP), both of which are reform movements that were created at the turn of the century. The Muslims are organized in the Muslim League.

TABLE II
COMMUNIST PARTY VOTE IN KERALA BY DISTRICT
(in per cent)

District	1957	1960	1965	1967[a]
Malabar	31.9	38.6	35.2	31.6
Cannanore	37.8	39.1	33.4	32.4
Kozhikode	17.1	22.9	23.4	21.2
Palghat	40.7	53.8	48.9	41.1
Cochin	32.7	38.4	22.9	37.4
Trichur	32.1	43.2	27.1	37.3
Ernakulam	42.9	31.5	20.3	34.6
Kottayam	23.1	40.6	21.3	40.4
Travancore	39.1	43.8	27.9	30.3
Alleppey	35.3	41.4	27.0	30.2
Quilon	41.2	42.7	28.5	34.1
Trivandrum	40.9	47.2	28.4	26.5

SOURCE: *Report on the Third General Elections in India, 1962*, Vol. II (Statistical), Election Commission, India.

[a]Includes both the CPI and the CPI [M].

The Communal Factor in Kerala

Politics in Kerala, particularly in the two southern districts of Travancore and Cochin, which were ruled by feudal princes during the British period, have for most of the past 100 years been based largely on communal loyalties. In Travancore-Cochin, an alliance developed in the 1880's between the Nairs and the low-caste Ezhavas; it was directed against the Brahmans, who were associated with the ruling Maharajah in the feudal order. The Nairs resented the Brahman prerogatives and, moreover, wanted social and religious reform in order to eliminate the matriarchal system, which deprived Nair males of the right to inherit the land owned by their fathers. The Nairs had no difficulty in mobilizing the Ezhavas against the Brahmans, since the Ezhavas had numerous religious and social grievances of their own: they were not admitted to government service or schools, were not allowed in temples, and so on.

By the 1930's, the situation had changed. The Nairs had replaced the Brahmans in the top political positions, and an alliance of Ezhavas, Christians, and Muslims had been formed against them. After India was granted independence, in 1947, the Congress Party came to power in Travancore-Cochin; because the Party was controlled by the Christians, a new alliance grew up: non-Christians against Christians. In 1956, still another constellation of forces developed. At this time, Travancore-Cochin was combined with Malabar to form the new Malayalam-speaking state of Kerala. Because of their preponderance in Malabar, the Ezhavas became, overnight, the largest single community in the state. Increasingly conscious of their own strength and resentful of their low social and economic status, they rallied around Communist leaders, many of whom were themselves Ezhavas. This was a major factor in the Communist electoral victory of 1957. The fragile nature of this victory was brought out two years later, when the Communist government was overthrown as a result of considerable popular unrest, in the so-called liberation struggle. This struggle was in part a Nair-Christian-Muslim alliance directed against the Ezhavas, whose Communist leaders, by pressing certain educational and economic reforms, threatened to disadvantage the other communal groups in the state.

In short, Kerala first saw a movement of all groups against the Brahmans, then a movement of non-Nairs against Nairs, then a movement of non-Christians against Christians, and, beginning in 1959, a movement of non-Ezhavas against Ezhavas. In each case, political cooperation grew out of the desire of the three less powerful groups to prevent the decisive dominance of the fourth.

In the 1965 elections, no single community was strong enough to bid for power, and splits developed in the ranks of each. Within the Congress Party, the division reflected smoldering Ezhava discontent with Christian domination. The rebel Congress forces were therefore able to pull a number of Ezhava votes away from the Communists. However, each of the political parties in Kerala continues to be dependent on certain communities. The Communists have the support of the Ezhavas and the Harijans; the Congress Party, of the Christians and the Nairs; the Socialists, of the Nairs; and the Muslim League, of the Muslims.

There is little doubt that much of the Communist strength in Kerala comes from the support of the Ezhavas. This strength may be measured in various ways. The main Communist stronghold in Kerala since the formation of the state has been the district of Palghat in Malabar, the only district in Kerala with an Ezhava majority. In the four State Legislative Assembly elections between 1957 and 1967, the Communists have consistently received more than 40 per cent of the vote in Palghat, a record unparalleled elsewhere in the state. Communist strength among the Ezhavas is also reflected in the large number of Ezhava candidates the Party puts up for election in Kerala. Finally, one writer has tested the relationship between party and community in electoral behavior in Kerala in the 1960 election, when the voting choice was unusually polarized between a pro- and anti-Communist grouping. The result was a .6 correlation between the Communists and the Ezhavas and scheduled castes.[16]

The relationship between the Communists and the Ezhavas in Kerala, however, is a marriage of convenience, not a permanent alliance. The Ezhavas look to the Communists to elevate their community socially and economically, and the Communists look to the Ezhavas for political support. Neither is entirely happy with the arrangement. Most of the Ezhava leaders in fact support the Congress Party, and the Communists would prefer a broader class base among the downtrodden than a community base which sets limits on their appeals to other communities.

As one writer pointed out, in describing the Communist-Ezhava relationship:

> Today the reform which the Ezhavas want is economic, and they have become convinced during the last decade [1952-62] that it is only through the K.C.P. [Kerala Communist Party] that they will secure it. The Ezhavas are a politically conscious group, aware of the issues and not easily swayed by slogans. For this reason they have been willing to support the K.C.P. in spite of the Congress orientation of their caste associations leaders. . . . Thus between the Ezhavas and the Communists there has been no fundamental meeting of minds, but rather a fortunate confluence of program and action. . . . The Communists, for their part, do not really think of the Ezhavas as the "proper" class for their support.[17]

The Congress Party puts up Christian candidates to a much greater extent than the Communist Party does and is also much more successful with its Christian candidates. As was indicated earlier, the principal reason for this phenomenon is that the Congress Party in Kerala has for some time been dominated by Christian bishops; consequently, the struggle between the two parties has been in part a struggle between Ezhavas and Christians. It was the Christian bishops and the leaders of the Nair Service Society who, together, led the 1959 liberation struggle that brought down the Communist government. More recently, there has been a split within the Congress Party on communal grounds, with the bulk of the Christians going over to the rebel Congress Party.

But Communism in Kerala is obviously more than a communal affair between the Ezhavas and the Harijans. Table III indicates that the Communist Party is stronger among Nairs than any other Kerala party except the P.S.P. It seems reasonable to assume, therefore, that the Kerala Communists have succeeded in obtaining the support of large numbers of the poor in Kerala, irrespective of community. Thus, Communism in Kerala is as much a class as a communal phenomenon.

At this point it is important to note that Kerala, as contrasted with the rest of India, particularly with northern and western India, has an abnormally high concentration of agricultural laborers, sharecroppers, and owners of dwarf holdings (those of one acre or less) in proportion to the total number of the peasantry (see Table III). The median ratio for agricultural laborers to total peasantry in India as a whole is 19.7 per cent. That is, on the average, about one out of five Indian cultivators is a hired laborer, as distinct from a tenant or owner-cultivator. In Kerala, by contrast, not one district has a laborer ratio of less than 30 per cent and two districts, Cannanore and Palghat, where the Communists are particularly strong, have a ratio of higher than 60 per cent. Thus, in both districts laborers outnumber other cultivators.

Tenancy figures for Kerala are also much higher than the average for India (about 80 per cent of tenancy takes the form of sharecropping). Table III shows the figures, by district, for "pure" tenancy, which in the 1961 Indian census is distinguished from "mixed" tenancy. Pure tenancy is

TABLE III
LANDLESSNESS IN KERALA

Region	Agricultural Laborers[a] (as per cent of all cultivators)	Pure Tenancy (as per cent of all landholdings)	Dwarf Holdings[b] (as per cent of all landholdings)
India	19.7	5.1	5.0
Malabar			
Cannanore	71.1	77.9	37.4
Palghat	60.8	79.6	21.8
Kozhikode	46.9	75.3	35.0
Cochin			
Trichur	47.9	62.8	33.0
Ernakulam	40.6	29.8	45.4
Kottayam	43.1	12.9	50.4
Travancore			
Alleppey	51.6	12.1	61.4
Quilon	30.2	5.6	58.5
Trivandrum	40.5	8.2	60.7

SOURCE: Government of India, *Census of India, 1961,* Vol. I, Part I-A (ii): *Levels of Regional Development in India.*

[a]The median for agricultural laborers is based on 296 districts; for pure tenancy, on 300 districts; and for dwarf holdings, on 299 districts. There are 336 districts in India, but data on some variables were not available from census publications.

[b]Those of one acre or less.

defined as land leased from private persons, whereas in the case of mixed tenancy the land is leased partly from the government and partly from private persons. The figures cited here have been confined to pure tenancy only because the figures for mixed tenancy were not readily available. The addition of these figures, however, would merely reinforce the fact that Kerala has the highest proportion of tenancy of any state in India. The figures for seven out of nine districts are at least double the Indian average. In Malabar (Cannanore, Kozhikode, and Palghat), tenancy accounts for 70 per cent or more of the landholdings in each of the three districts, as opposed to an Indian average of 5.1 per cent. Malabar has consistently been the region of greatest Communist strength in Kerala, particularly in the Cannanore and Palghat districts, which, as has been seen, are also very high in laborers.

Finally, as Table III also indicates, Kerala is also abnormally high in dwarf holdings. Every district in Kerala has a dwarf-holding ratio of more than 20 per cent as contrasted with an Indian average of 5 per cent. These figures are not mutually exclusive. That is, an agricultural laborer may also be a sharecropping tenant on someone else's land or he may own a small piece of land. About 50 per cent of India's agricultural laborers own tiny pieces of land. What these figures suggest, then, is that Kerala has an extraordinarily high concentration of agricultural laborers who are also sharecroppers and/or owners of dwarf holdings. Such "propertied" or sharecropping laborers are more independent than are completely propertyless laborers and, therefore, are more susceptible to radicalization.[18] One possible reason for this may be the ambivalence of the position of this propertied proletariat; for the incongruity in status between owning land, sharecropping, and hiring out one's labor is perceived rather sharply by individuals who do all three, as opposed to individuals who are completely propertyless.

In addition to a propertied proletariat, Kerala also has the largest concentration of plantation workers of any state in India. There are nineteen districts in India with more than 10,000 workers on tea, coffee, and rubber plantations; all nine districts of Kerala are included in this category. This rural proletariat, working under factory-like conditions on plantations and farms, is easier to radicalize than dispersed rural workers, for a variety of reasons. Communications and organization are easier; there is strength and confidence in numbers; and the factory-like conditions proletarianize the peasant and make him more class conscious.

Although no systematic study has been made to demonstrate conclusively that class factors cut into community loyalties to determine voting allegiance in Kerala, there is one example that is suggestive. In Mankada, a heavily Muslim constituency in Palghat, the Communist Muslim candidate has easily defeated his Muslim League rivals in several elections. In the neighboring district of Kozhikode, however, Muslim League candidates are much more successful against Communist candidates. The reason for this seems to be that Mankada Muslims are largely agricultural laborers, whereas in Kozhikode there is a greater concentration of middle-class Muslims engaged in trade and commerce. In short, it seems that the Communists do better among Muslim agricultural laborers than they do among middle-class Muslims. This is probably also true for the other communities.

If the existence of a large number of agricultural laborers and plantation workers provides the environmental, or "objective," condition for Communist success in Kerala, it is the Nair and Ezhava leadership that provides the "subjective" prerequisite for that success. As Table IV indicates, twelve out of eighteen top Communist leaders in Kerala (including both the left-wing and right-wing parties) are high-caste Hindus; that is, Brahmans, Nairs, or other high castes. Nine out of eighteen are Nairs, who are in many ways the dominant caste in Kerala. It is this indigenous high-caste Hindu leadership, most of which comes from the country-side, that has obviously played a key role in mobilizing large sections of the Kerala peasantry behind the Communists. The importance of this indigenous leadership can be gauged by noting the rough correlation between the regions of Kerala from which the Communist leadership originally sprung and the strength of the Party today. Both E. M. S. Namboodiripad and A. K. Gopalan, the two most prominent Kerala Communist leaders, come from Malabar. The Cochin and Travancore Communist parties were offshoots of the Malabar Communist Party.

At the middle levels of Communist Party leadership,

TABLE IV
COMMUNITY AFFILIATION OF LEADERS
OF THE LEFT-WING AND RIGHT-WING
COMMUNIST PARTIES IN KERALA[a]

Community Affiliation	Left-wing Leaders	Right-wing Leaders
Brahman	1	0
Nair	2	7
High-caste Hindu (other than Brahman or Nair)	0	2
Ezhava	2	1
Harijan	1	0
Muslim	1	1

SOURCE: Biographical data gathered by the author on the basis of interviews conducted in India in 1965.

[a]Central Committee and National Council members, respectively.

Ezhavas and Nairs are just about evenly divided. (Candidates for the State Legislative Assembly are often leaders of the Party at the district level.) The pattern of leadership suggests that the Nairs dominate the top ranks of the Communist leadership in Kerala and that the Nairs and Ezhavas together constitute the middle ranks.

This provides another key to Communist success in Kerala; for in Indian conditions it is generally impossible for any party to mobilize the countryside unless its leadership is rooted in a dominant caste.

Organization is still another factor that must be taken into account in explaining the success of the Communists in Kerala. The importance of organization in underdeveloped countries, in particular, should not be underestimated. The authors of one major study of Indian voting behavior have shown that in one constituency that they scrutinized closely, there was not one voting booth in the constituency in which the Congress Party did not get at least 20 per cent of the total votes cast. They attributed this to the Party's organizational skill (see note 10). In Kerala, about one-third of the total population is working class if one adds urban workers and agricultural laborers together. Some 50 per cent of this group are organized in trade unions, many of which are under Communist influence. On an all-India basis, only about 20 per cent of the urban working class, and a negligible proportion of the agricultural laborers, are organized. (The influence of trade unions in radicalizing workers and peasants has been stressed by Hamilton; see note 6.)

In sum, the "objective" reason for Communism's greater strength in Kerala than anywhere else in India seems to lie in the existence of a large, highly concentrated, low-caste rural proletariat, in the form of agricultural laborers, sharecroppers, owners of dwarf holdings, and plantation workers. The "subjective" factor contributing to Communist success in Kerala is the existence of an upper-caste, indigenous leadership that has been able to mobilize and organize that rural proletariat.

Communism Outside of Kerala

Let us now briefly examine the social base of Communism elsewhere in India, particularly in terms of the uprootedness, communalism, and class theories. West Bengal, along with Kerala and Andhra Pradesh, gave the Communists more than 20 per cent of the vote in the 1962 elections. This was in sharp contrast to the generally poor performance of the Communists elsewhere in India, indicating that Indian Communism is a regional, rather than a national, phenomenon.

But the social base of Bengali Communism is substantially different from that in Kerala and Andhra Pradesh. Communist strength in West Bengal is more evenly divided between urban and rural areas than in Kerala and Andhra Pradesh, where it is largely rural. In West Bengal, in the 1962 elections, seventeen out of fifty Communist members of the State Legislative Assembly, or approximately one-third, came from urban constituencies, whereas in Kerala eleven out of forty-three, and in Andhra Pradesh three out of fifty-one, came from urban constituencies. In Kerala and Andhra Pradesh, the only highly urbanized districts, Trivandrum and Hyderabad respectively, have comparatively little Communist strength, whereas in the sprawling Bengali metropolis of Calcutta Communist strength is impressive. Out of twenty-six State Legislative Assembly seats in the Calcutta constituencies in the 1962 elections, the Communists contested eighteen and won eight; in all but three they contested, they received more than 40 per cent of the vote.

In the urban areas of West Bengal, Communist strength does not appear to be based on any particular caste or community. Rather, one of the main bases seems to be the several million "declassed" Hindu refugees who fled their homes in East Bengal after partition. These refugees constitute about one-fourth of the West Bengal population and a substantial portion of the Calcutta population. They apparently vote for the Communists overwhelmingly.

Here, it would seem, is a classic example of uprooted and declassed individuals supporting an extremist party in accordance with the model put forth by the proponents of the concept of mass society. The uprootedness of the Hindu refugees in Calcutta is aggravated by the fact that many of them occupied positions of considerable power and influence in East Bengal, but are denied power or status in West Bengal. The absence of an effective and large Jana Sangh in Calcutta is probably the main reason why the Hindu refugees there have chosen left-wing rather than right-wing extremism. At least one Communist leader frankly admitted to the author that many of the followers of his party in Calcutta were the kind of declassed petty bourgeois who in the North belonged to the militantly communal Hindu party, the Jana Sangh.

To some extent, however, Communist strength in Calcutta is also based on both community and class. West Bengal has a large number of immigrants from other parts of India—

particularly from Bihar, Gujarat, and other states in the North—who migrate to Calcutta seeking employment. These immigrants appear to vote in accordance with the political traditions of the regions from which they have come. Thus, the non-Bengalis from northern India, particularly the Biharis and Gujaratis, generally vote for the Congress Party, regardless of class. In fact, even a large majority of non-Bengali workers vote for the Congress Party. In 1957, according to *New Age*, the Communist Party weekly, the left-wing parties combined, including the Communists, were unable to poll more than 10 per cent of the non-Bengali working-class vote.[19] Several Communist officials told the author that even non-Bengali workers belonging to Communist-led trade unions generally voted for the Congress Party. As a result, the Bengali Communists have been forced to seek support largely from indigenous Bengalis, who constitute a minority of the labor force in Calcutta.

The voting pattern of the non-Bengalis can only be explained on regional grounds. Those from the North believe that the Congress Party "looks after" the northern Indian, Hindi-speaking belt with which they continue to identify after moving to West Bengal. By the same token, southern Indians in Calcutta—particularly those from Kerala, but also non-Hindi-speaking southerners in general—are more susceptible to the Communists, who are not identified with the Hindi-speaking North. So predictable are the political loyalties of these immigrant communities in Calcutta that Communist election workers have instructions to ignore Gujaratis and Marwaris, to be skeptical about Biharis, and to concentrate on southern Indians and Bengalis of all classes. Thus, even in the urban melting pot of Calcutta, community loyalties based on the linguistic and cultural gulf dividing northern from southern India are politically of enormous significance. Whereas indigenous Bengalis are divided along class lines, non-Bengalis seem to be divided more along communal lines.

Andhra Pradesh, the third state in which the Communists have substantial strength, can be divided into three regions: the fertile Delta areas, which are largely agricultural; the arid Rayalaseema region; and the former princely state of Hyderabad, which in 1956 was joined with the Telugu-speaking portions of Madras to form the linguistic state of Andhra Pradesh. Communist strength in Andhra Pradesh is largely confined to the Delta areas and to the sections of Hyderabad that are commonly called Telingana. In the 1962 elections, the Communists secured forty of their fifty-one seats from these two areas. Their leadership is also drawn largely from these two areas. Out of a total of twenty-two top leaders of both the right and left wings of the Communist Party in Andhra Pradesh, seven are from Telingana, thirteen from the Delta, and only two from Rayalaseema, where the Congress Party has a firm stronghold.

Communist strength in the Delta is such that, as early as 1946, it was the only region in India where the Communists felt strong enough to enter candidates in a large contiguous group of constituencies against candidates of the Congress Party—who were champions of Indian independence at a time when India remained under foreign domination.[20]

To have roots in a dominant local caste, then, may be necessary to the Communists. But it does not sufficiently explain Communist strength in the Delta. Any explanation of this phenomenon must take into account that, as Table V indicates, the concentration of agricultural laborers there, most of whom are Harijans, is second in all of India only to that of Malabar. And, as in Kerala generally and in Malabar in particular, many of these laborers are also owners of dwarf holdings.

The strength of Communism in Telingana, however, is

TABLE V
LANDLESSNESS IN ANDHRA PRADESH

Region	Agricultural Laborers (as per cent of all cultivators)	Pure Tenancy (as per cent of all landholdings)	Dwarf Holdings[a] (as per cent of all landholdings)
Delta	47.2	6.1	14.8
Rayalaseema	39.6	5.3	8.4
Telingana	39.5	5.9	8.7
Andhra Pradesh	39.6	5.3	11.9
India	19.7	5.1	5.0

SOURCE: Same as Table III.

[a]Those of one acre or less.

more difficult to relate to high ratios of agricultural laborers, tenants, or owners of dwarf holdings. As Table V points up, Telingana is very close to the Andhra Pradesh state average in all three categories, although it is double the Indian average in ratio of agricultural laborers to peasants. Historical factors are probably of crucial importance in explaining Communist success in Telingana. It was in these areas that the Communists in 1946 led a "national" and social struggle. The national struggle was for merging the Telugu-speaking parts of Hyderabad with the Telugu-speaking parts of Madras to form the linguistic region of Andhra. The social struggle was on behalf of the rural poor, most of whom were Hindus, against the large Muslim landlords, who had the support of the Muslim Nizam. The Communists stirred up the grievances of the poor Hindu peasantry by combining economic, religious, and linguistic demands.

Thus, the common denominator of Communist success in both Kerala and Andhra Pradesh seems to lie in the existence of an unusually large and highly concentrated rural proletariat that is mobilized by an indigenous upper-caste Communist leadership on the basis of combined linguistic and social demands. This combination of a social base among poor peasants and subnational demands is important, because one without the other seems ineffective. In Maharashtra, for example, the Communists got behind a linguistic movement in 1957, but were swamped at the polls in 1962 and 1967 because they had no rural base.

Outside their strongholds in Kerala, West Bengal, and Andhra Pradesh, the Indian Communists have only pockets of influence. Most of these are in rural areas. In the 1962 elections in Bihar, the Communists won twelve State Legislative Assembly seats, ten of which were in rural constituencies. In Maharashtra, four of their six seats were in rural areas; in the Punjab, all nine seats were in rural areas; in Uttar Pradesh, ten out of fourteen were rural. Thus, with the exception of its strength in Calcutta and in certain trade unions in Andhra Pradesh, Maharashtra, and other industrialized states, Indian Communism is a rural phenomenon.

The view that Indian Communism is largely a rural phenomenon is confirmed by several other observations. Out of forty-five Indian cities with populations of over 200,000 the Communists contested more than half of the State Legislative Assembly seats in only fifteen, and won only slightly less than 10 per cent of those they contested. Even in as important an industrial and commercial city as Bombay, where they have a foothold in the trade unions, the Communists contested only ten out of twenty-four seats and won only one.

The Social Basis of the Communist Party Split

It remains to say a few words about the left-right split in the Indian Communist Party, a split that, as suggested earlier, cannot be adequately understood without considering its social basis.* The right-wing Communists have their main base in the All-India Trade Union Congress (AITUC), the Communist-dominated trade-union federation. The left-wing Communists have their main base in the All-India Kisan Sabha (AIKS), the Communist-dominated peasant movement. Out of thirty-five right-wing leaders in Andhra Pradesh, West Bengal, and Kerala, fifteen are leaders of the AITUC. Out of nineteen left-wing leaders in the same three states, only three are trade-union leaders. On the other hand, seven out of nineteen left-wing leaders are active in the Kisan movement, whereas only seven out of thirty-five right-wing leaders are similarly active. The strength of the right-wing Communists in the trade unions is symbolized by the fact that their head, S. A. Dange, is a Bombay trade-union leader. The prominent leaders of the left-wing Communists, on the other hand, are men who are rooted in the peasant movement, such as A. K. Gopalan in Kerala and N. Prasada Rao in Andhra Pradesh.

The AITUC seems to be a more conservative interest group in the Indian Communist Party than is the AIKS, possibly because trade-union leaders have a natural tendency to stress economic rather than political demands.

A point of equal importance is that the left-wing Communist leadership in the three states is made up to a much greater extent of individuals of lower class and caste than is the right-wing leadership. In West Bengal, all nine right-wing leaders are Brahmans, Kaists, or Vaidyas, the three dominant castes in West Bengal, whereas none of the three left-wing leaders for whom information is available belong to any of these castes. Two of the left-wing leaders are Muslims. In Kerala, there are proportionately more Ezhavas than Nairs in

*The right and left wings of the Indian Communist Party are, respectively, the Communist Party of India (CPI) and the Communist Party of India-Marxist (CPI[M]). More recently, an ultra-left third party has appeared, the Naxalburi group, which preaches rural revolution. Subsequent references to the "left" include both the CPM and the Naxalburi group.

the left-wing Communist leadership. The left-wing leaders in that state—and in others—tend to be lower class, less well educated, and without a fluent command of English. The right-wing leaders are higher class, much better educated, and more fluent in English. It is symptomatic that almost all the English-educated Communists—graduates of Cambridge, Oxford, the London School of Economics—belong to the right wing of the Party. Many of these, who come from prosperous middle-class and upper-caste families, are resented by their lower-class "comrades." As one disgruntled Communist put it, "You have to have a Cambridge degree to get anywhere in the Party." The recent resignation from the Party of Mohan Kumaramangalam—the son of a former Indian Civil Service official, of high-caste origin, English educated, and a prominent and fairly wealthy Madras lawyer in his own right—was in part a result of the continuing campaign conducted against him by "comrades" from more humble backgrounds.

The "class" division in the Party was institutionalized when the Communists found it necessary to send representatives to Parliament. Generally they chose well-educated candidates who were fluent in English. This inevitably led to friction between the parliamentary and the organizational wings of the Party, since the latter's leaders were generally of more humble origins, less well educated, and often anti-intellectual. Typical of such differences prior to the split was the situation in West Bengal, where urbane, cosmopolitan, English-educated leaders like Renu Chakravarty and Indrajeet Gupta represented the Party in Parliament, whereas the organizational machinery was controlled by Promode Das Gupta, a man of limited education and rural origins. When the split came, Das Gupta joined the left-wing Communists and Gupta and Chakravarty entered the right wing.

Thus, pressures for radicalization within the Communist Party seem to be coming, not unnaturally, from leaders of lower class and caste rather than from those of higher class and caste. This is not to make a simple and direct correlation between caste or class and political inclination. Nevertheless, there are a number of factors—including caste, class, education, region, revolutionary experience—that seem to produce proclivities toward moderation or extremism among Communist leaders. Education seems to be particularly important. The educational level of the right-wing leaders is considerably higher at the top of the Party than that of the left-wing leaders. For example, seven out of nine West Bengal right-wing leaders, but only one out of five left-wing leaders, have college or advanced degrees. In Andhra Pradesh, six out of fifteen right-wing leaders, but only two out of seven left-wing leaders, hold college degrees.

Moreover, there are quite a few "pure" left- and right-wing leaders, that is, leaders who fit all or most of various criteria. The pure left-wing leader, for example, would be of low caste and class background, have a low educational level, be unable to speak English fluently, and work in the peasant movement. The pure right-wing leader, on the other hand, would be of high caste and class, have a high educational level, be a fluent English speaker, and work in the trade-union movement and/or Parliament.

Conclusions

Of the various theories to explain the appeal of Communism that have been tested on the Indian Communist Party, the communalism and class concepts would seem to be of greater utility than the theory of uprootedness. There is, however, no simple and direct relationship between communalism and Communism or between class and Communism. Communalism can, under certain circumstances, be either an obstacle or an opportunity for the Communists. Nowhere can the effect of communalism on Communism's fortunes be properly assessed without taking into account other factors, particularly class. In most areas where the Communists are strong, they have succeeded in mobilizing the downtrodden, particularly the landless laborers in the countryside; but they have not been able to mobilize the rural poor in most parts of India. The most potent appeal comes from a blending of communal, class, and subnational demands.

Notes

1. William Kornhauser, *The Politics of Mass Society* (Glencoe, 1959), pp. 158 and 163.
2. Adam B. Ulam, *The Unfinished Revolution* (New York, 1960).
3. Richard Lowenthal, "The Totalitarian Revolutions of Our Time," a series of lectures written for Radio Free Europe in 1965.
4. Seymour M. Lipset, *Political Man: The Social Bases of Politics* (New York, 1959), p. 136.
5. Erik Allardt, "Patterns of Class Conflict and Working Class Consciousness in Finnish Politics," in Erik Allardt and Yrjö Littunen (eds.), *Cleavages, Ideologies and Party Systems* (Helsinki, 1964), p. 128.
6. Juan J. Linz, "The Social Bases of West German Politics" (unpublished doctoral dissertation, Columbia University, 1959); Seymour M. Lipset, *Political Man* (New York, 1960); William Kornhauser, *The Politics of Mass Society* (New York, 1959); Richard Hamilton, *Affluence and the French Worker in the 4th Republic* (Princeton, 1967). For a survey of the literature on working-class radicalism, see Leslie Schuster, "Occupational Radicalism and the Miners of Chile" (term paper, Hunter College, Fall, 1968).
7. These phenomena will be explored in my forthcoming book, *The Social Sources of Peasant Radicalism.* For some of the relevant literature, and for many suggestive insights, I have profited from an unpublished paper by Juan Linz, "Patterns of Land Tenure and Division of Labor and Politics."
8. See Donald S. Zagoria, "Communism in Asia," *Commentary,* XXXIX, No. 2 (February, 1965), for an outline of the communal theory.
9. Some writers employ the term "communalism" to denote particular kinds of parochial loyalties; others use it more broadly. Myron Weiner(*The Politics of Scarcity: Public Pressure and Political Response in India* [Chicago, 1962], p. 37) suggests that "community associations constitute one type of associational interest. A distinction can be made between voluntary associations and those formed ascriptively, that is, whether the grouping is joined voluntarily or whether it is one into which an individual is born. Among the former associations are those based upon class and occupational distinctions: trade unions, business associations, peasant organizations—and one might also include refugees and students; among the latter are religious, tribal, caste and linguistic associations." In this study, the term "communalism" will be used in the latter sense, i.e., an associational group into which an individual is born.

10. See the "Baroda East" study by Rajni Kothari and Tarun Sheth, in Myron Weiner and Rajni Kothari (eds.), *Indian Voting Behavior* (London, 1965).
11. For further amplification, see Donald S. Zagoria, "Asia," *Survey* (London), No. 54 (January, 1965), pp. 89-104.
12. C. von Fürer-Haimendorf, "Caste and Politics in South Asia," in C. H. Philips (ed.), *Politics and Society in India* (New York, 1963), p. 68.
13. See the articles by Bernard B. Fall and Leo E. Rose, in Robert A. Scalapino (ed.), *The Communist Revolution in Asia: Tactics, Goals, and Achievements* (Englewood Cliffs, 1965).
14. Valerian Gracias, "The Challenge of Kerala," *Mission Bulletin* XI, No. 8 (October, 1959), 761.
15. I have profited from a paper by Stephen Oren on the political role of Kerala's Christians.
16. Michael St. John, "The Communist Party and Communal Politics in Kerala" (senior honors thesis, Department of Social Relations, Harvard University, 1962), cited in Lloyd I. Rudolph and Susanne H. Rudolph, *The Modernity of Traditions* (Chicago, 1967), p. 72.
17. *Ibid.*
18. I am indebted to an unpublished paper by Juan Linz for this observation.
19. See Selig S. Harrison, *India: The Most Dangerous Decades* (Princeton, 1960), p. 201.
20. *Ibid.*

IV

BUDDHISM AS A POLITICAL FACTOR IN SOUTHEAST ASIA

Emanuel Sarkisyanz

All the Buddhist countries of the so-called Little Vehicle regained their independence (which Thailand had never lost) after World War II. In Ceylon and Burma, Buddhism again became an important political factor. That Buddhism has played and does play a political role is an insight not easily reconcilable with the image of that philosophy as popularized by classical Indology, or with the utilitarian notion that philosophical abstractions cannot be relevant to concrete political problems. Thus the great Indologist S. F. Oldenburg refused to recognize the vitality and historical power of the modernistic political reinterpretations of Buddhism that arose in response to occidental rule and to the development of the Southeast Asian economies without the participation of the Buddhist peoples of the area. Subsequent experts, less burdened with the history of ideas, have followed in the refusal to take such a striking phenomenon as Buddhist-Marxist syncretism very seriously, on the assumption *dass nicht sein kann, was nicht sein darf* (that it cannot be because it should not be). Buddhism is considered to be the concern of historians of religion, theologians, and orientalists, while

Marxism is an object of study for economists, political scientists, and area specialists.

Thus it happened that serious experts raised the question of whether Buddhism was compatible with Marxism. The question is unhistorical and of nominalistic relevance at best—about as relevant as the question of whether Hegelianism was compatible with the Jacobin revolutionary tradition. (The fact is that Marx *did* combine them.) Nevertheless, the compatibility question has long distracted research from the more realistic problem of the historical conditions for Buddhist-Marxist syncretism. The latter has for a considerable time been a political fact. But investigation of its intellectual history has been obstructed by the identification of the whole of Theravada Buddhism with the otherworldly monastic tradition of the Pali canon. As this canonic Theravada Buddhism did actually de-emphasize society and worldly life, the popularizations of Indology have long created the impression that no form of Buddhist thought could possibly have produced a political ethos.

The Tradition of Secular Buddhism

It is true that the Buddhist monastic order, as an institution, was not meant to act politically. Only minorities within it have ever been politically active, and generally only in times of crisis. Yet at the same time, the ethos of the Buddhist monastic order has long been the political ideal of Buddhist lay society: in the ideal Buddhist future, state and society are to dissolve into a monastic order with a community of property. It is true that Buddhist ethics does not condemn the acquisition of property by laymen. But it is more decisive that Theravada Buddhism has not sanctified individual acquisition, as has Calvinist Protestantism. Of course, the main object of the Buddha's message was not the transformation of society. But even early Buddhist canonic

texts contain descriptions of an ideal Buddhist society whose
social harmony facilitates ethical conduct and, ultimately,
the pursuit of nirvana. Although the final goal of the
Buddhist way is nirvana, a large part of the Buddhist canon
does not deal with this final goal but with the social
environment that would best serve to facilitate its attain-
ment.

This applies even more to Buddhisms other than the
canonic Buddhism the Indologist usually had in mind when
referring to that world religion: politically no less relevant are
the partly animistic folk-Buddhisms of the various Theravada
countries, and particularly the historical lay Buddhist values
of medieval Southeast Asian epigraphy by which secular
rulers since antiquity have professed a Buddhist ethos of
kingship and attempted to justify their power in terms of
Buddhist morality. Those are the Buddhist ideals of state that
folklore has kept alive subhistorically into the twentieth
century. That "Asokan" historical lay Buddhism is more
relevant to Buddhist political thought than is the monastic
Buddhism of the canon is usually overlooked. That even the
primeval canonic Buddhism is mutable is nowadays affirmed
by both traditionalist monks and Marxist syncretists. Those
who reject Buddhism's historical departures from its original
forms represent, in fact, an unhistorical rationalism: their
interpretation of the original tradition demands a strict
consistency which even the canon hardly had. Thus the
notion of karma, of causation's fruits from previous lives, is
sometimes used against Buddhist arguments for radical social
reforms; yet even the medieval Buddhist rulers of Ceylon and
Burma invoked karma in the same breath as they proclaimed
economic welfare measures to alleviate human suffering.

The historiography of both Ceylon and Burma attributes
to the Buddha himself prophecies on the destiny of those
lands. Traditionally, Ceylon saw itself as the "Island of the
Buddhist Law" (Dhammadipa). Ceylon's sense of mission

grew out of the certainty that it had been chosen by the Buddha himself to become the preserver of the pure Theravada teachings, the land from which the monastic order and the lay community of Buddhism were to radiate into the known world. The belief that the Buddha had sanctified Ceylon by his alleged visit—and thus prepared the island for its glorious future—has largely shaped the self-image of the Sinhalese people, just as the concept of the island from which Theravada Buddhism was to spread has strongly influenced the historical self-image of Burma. Burmese peasants still think of Buddha as a fellow Burman. Even in her wars against fellow Buddhists in Thailand, Burma looked on Ceylon's defensive wars against non-Buddhist Brahmanic conquerors from Southern India as models. Burma's rulers, like those of Ceylon, claimed descent from Buddha's family.

At the same time, the kings derived themselves from the "First Ruler," who was believed to have been freely elected by men when the mythical primitive state of communal property (in which harvests grew by themselves, without human labor) had vanished. It was then that the aberration of selfishness produced private property, class differences, social conflict, and thereby the necessity for a ruler. The tradition of an initial social utopia, its subsequent loss, and the origin of the state through a kind of social contract, as a result of conflicts over property, is contained in one of the earliest sections of the Buddhist canon. This "social contract" theory of kingship has been described as a Buddhist contribution to Indian political theory.

On the other hand, the small republican commonwealths of early Buddhist northern India may have stimulated the semi-"republican" canonic structure of the Buddhist monastic community (just as Roman imperial patterns of centralized authority may have stimulated the hierarchical organization of the early Christian Church).

Subsequently, political and social stratification in the historic Indic monarchies were rationalized by folk-Buddhistic notions about rebirth in a social station corresponding to the moral merit acquired in previous lives. The charisma of political power came to be seen as a moral obligation from the time of the ideal Buddhist ruler Asoka. This first unifier of the Indian subcontinent, in the middle of the third century B.C., did, at the height of his military power, publicly regret and renounce conquest by violence, proclaiming that he desired to conquer only through the power of Buddhist morality. Asoka wanted to be remembered for having planted gardens and built water tanks and shelters with the purpose of making it easier for men to observe the moral law of dharma. Though his inscriptions have subsequently been forgotten, the Asoka legend has transmitted his vision of a Buddhist welfare state throughout Buddhist lands. It is echoed in the *Mahavamsa,* for example, which says of King Mahinda II (772-92): "The poor who were ashamed to beg he supported in secret, and there were none in the island who were not supported by him."

An examination of historical (as distinguished from canonical) Buddhism thus does not bear out Max Weber's contention that there is no bridge between the Buddhist ideal and active social endeavor. Buddhism denies reality to the concept of "mineness" (*mamatta*). The basic notions of "my," "this is I," "this is myself" are seen as devoid of reality. Attachment to attributes of mineness is to be overcome. Consciousness of the self as doer of a deed is considered an illusion. Therefore, the power of one individual over others cannot be fully rationalized in Buddhist terms. If it is possible, nevertheless, to derive an *ideal* vision of political rule from Buddhist ethics, it is precisely because the "non-substantiality of mineness" implies an aspiration to fulfill the basic oneness of one's "self" and other selves. The non-distinction between the happiness and sorrow of "others" and that of "one's self" is called *karuna.* It means the widening of consciousness to the point where it embraces all living beings, just as the Bodhisattva, the potential Buddha, was to renounce his own salvation until all beings had been saved. It was largely through the Bodhisattva ethos that "Buddhism developed . . . into one of the politically most effective ethical systems in the world," as Paul Mus wrote.[1] By the boundlessness of his abnegation, the Bodhisattva's kingly powers over others were to merge with the quest for their salvation from the fetters of illusory "mineness."

Ceylon

Though the Bodhisattva ideal developed mainly in Mahayana Buddhism, it also entered the Theravada Buddhism of Ceylon and Burma, beginning as a royal cult in the sixth century, down to the present on the level of folk religion. An inscription from the turn of the millennium explicitly declares that only Bodhisattvas could become rulers of Ceylon. This was believed until the British annexed the last independent state of Ceylon, in 1815. To its penultimate King of Kandy were still attributed the saintly virtues of that Bodhisattva who had refused to defend his state against aggressors—though it was by no means Buddhist pacifism that brought Ceylon under British domination.

British foreign rule soon came to be seen as an infringement of Buddhism. The British authorities eventually withdrew the traditional state support of the Buddhist monastic community—not without pressure from Protestant missionaries. A memorandum of the British missionary Spence Hardy based the necessity of destroying Buddhism "upon the simple fact that it is opposed to *the* truth," because Buddhism is nontheistic and hence "ignorant" of the missionaries' "*only* way of salvation by faith."[2] To his

Protestant Old-Testamentary zeal, the alleged "idolatry" of Buddhism was sufficient reason for seeking to destroy its beliefs. Typical of such Protestant missionary attitudes was the eager hope that Buddhism could be extinguished in one way or another, and that its eradication in Ceylon would be followed by its disappearance throughout the world; thus, in Britain, "with an increase of national influence arose the breath of prayer to heaven, that it might be exerted for the entire destruction of the empire of hell."[3]

It is understandable, then, that the early Ceylonese attempts to overthrow British rule (for example, in 1848) invoked the Buddhist heritage. By contrast, Christianity was accepted by those Ceylonese secular elites that became acculturated during the centuries of Portuguese, Dutch, and British domination. Largely descendants of the upper (Goyigama) class, they remained both culturally and sociologically separated from the Buddhist masses, even after receiving governmental authority from Britain between 1931 and 1947. The Goyigama are a privileged class even within the largest and most influential ordination school of Ceylon's Buddhist monasteries (the Ayudhia Nikaya, which has been influenced by Hindu caste patterns). Therefore, opposition to the Anglicized elite stimulated both a militant Buddhist revival among the masses and conflicts within Ceylonese Buddhism. A Buddhist monks' association, the Sri Lanka Maha Sangha Sabha, blamed Westernized, Anglicized elite rule for the decline of Buddhism: an election poster of 1956 showed Buddha being attacked by the English-style ruling premier and by an Uncle Sam, complete with dollar sign.

Since the Catholic minority, which under the Portuguese had persecuted Buddhism, still exercises economic and political influence out of all proportion to its numerical strength, the Marxist attack on Catholicism's Western associations was combined with communalistic, conservative appeals to the underprivileged Buddhist majority. Hence none of the

Marxist parties of Ceylon attacked Buddhism: even when
orthodox Communists criticized the demand for a Buddhist
state religion, they did so in Buddhist terms.

A militant use of Marxist arguments for Buddhist apologetics, as developed in Buddhist modernism since the turn of
the century, may be found in the book *Revolt in the Temple
or the Triumph of Righteousness*, published in 1953:
"British imperialism has been the *Māra* [Evil One] of
Buddhism; in its short career of 150 years it has destroyed
more Buddhist kingdoms than any other single agency had
done during the last 2,500 years. . . . In their greedy quest of
material wealth, they destroyed the Buddhist kingdoms, the
guideposts on mankind's path of happiness; now the de-
stroyers themselves are lost in the wilderness." In the context
of the "revolt in the temple," democracy is a "leaf from the
book of Buddhism, which has . . . been torn out and, while
perhaps not misread, has certainly been half emptied of
meaning by being divorced from its Buddhist context and
thus has been made subservient to reactionary forces. The
democracies today are obviously living on spiritual capital;
we mean clinging to the formal observances of Buddhism
without possessing its inner dynamic." Marxism is "a leaf
taken from the book of Buddhism—a leaf torn out and
misread." " 'Buddha is not content with taking away a man's
property and giving it to another. That is patchwork, like
social service,' writes Bhikkhu Dhammapala: 'Buddhism takes
away from people their instinct of possessiveness.' "

In the 1950's, militant Buddhists of Ceylon allied themselves with Marxists (whose main Ceylonese party, the Lanka
Sama Samaj, expelled the Stalinists and adopted a Trotskyite
orientation after the Hitler-Stalin Pact). Their alliance supported S. W. R. D. Bandaranaike, whose platform sought to
combine political democracy and economic socialism, as a
kind of "middle path" in the spirit of Buddhist ethics.
Bandaranaike was identified with the ideal Buddhist ruler of

the future and was even assigned the qualities of a Bodhisattva, which alone used to legitimate a ruler of Ceylon. Through his electoral victory of 1956, the Buddhist renovation movement contributed to Ceylon's neutralism and to the following nine years of the government's "leftist" economic policies. The socialist trend in economics thus combined with traditionalist, restorative tendencies in the cultural sphere.

Such nativistic revivalism and belief in a world-saving mission coincided in Ceylon with the middle of the third millennium after Buddha (celebrated in 1956) and the prophecies associated therewith: an age of Buddhist grandeur, a renovation of Buddhism, and the spread of its moral law throughout the world, was expected to begin—a golden age, as predicted for the coming of the future Buddha Maitreya (Mettaya). At its advent, sevenfold crops are again to appear without labor, the sick are to become healthy and the poor rich.

Burma

In Burma, the Buddhist tradition has bequeathed contradictory elements to the present age—an ideal of Asokan kingship on one hand, an ideal of the renunciation of worldly power on the other. Burma's King Kyanzittha of Pagan (1084-1112) proclaimed that he had had tanks built and groves planted, "only that all beings might escape out of samsara." Good harvests were to be assured through the king's (pre-Buddhist) fertility magic. This in turn contributed to state control over the agricultural economy: Burma's kings, lords of the "rain producing" White Elephant, were, at least formally, owners of a large part of all arable land. The Buddhist rulers were to feed the people every six months (*purisamedha*) and to lend funds to insolvent debtors or even to remit their debts. The ideal state of Asokan Buddhism would ensure such economic welfare as would permit the leisure necessary for meditation to pursue nirvana. Buddha is said to have postponed preaching about the impermanence of material satisfactions until his listener was fed: "If I preach the Law while he is suffering from the pangs of hunger, he will not be able to comprehend. . . . As soon as the poor man's physical suffering became relieved, his mind became tranquil. Then the Teacher preached the Law. . . . The poor man was established in the truth of conversion." Thus could Kyanzittha, one of the most renowned Burmese kings, proclaim:

> As by the Lord Buddha was foretold, so has all come to pass. . . . The bar of the gate of Heaven . . . by wisdom . . . [the] king shall draw open for [all mankind?] . The tears . . . by a course of benevolence . . . shall [the] king . . . wipe away. . . . Even the poor old women who sell pots . . . shall become rich . . . those who lack cattle shall have plenty of cattle . . . even poor people who have difficulty in getting food and clothes . . . [the king] . . . shall enrich them all . . . with his right hand he shall give boiled rice and bread to all the people, with his left hand he shall give ornaments and wearing apparel to all men. . . . When the king of the Law shall preach the Law, the sounds of applause of all men [shall be] like the sound of a rainstorm at the end of the year.

Though professing such Buddhist aspirations, many of Burma's rulers conquered by methods of blood and iron. A Burmese proverb includes Rulers among the Five Enemies (*yan-dhu-myou: nga: pa:*), together with Fire, Thieves, and Pestilence. In his past life, the subsequent Buddha took upon himself endless suffering only to avoid becoming king. The famous Ananda pagoda of Pagan is decorated with illustrations from that Jataka legend in which he reflected: "If I become king, I shall be born in hell. . . . My father through being a king is becoming guilty of grievous action which brings men to hell." That the *pragma* of power with its standards of political expediency was an obstacle to Buddhist renunciation and detachment was confirmed by the historical experience of the Burmese people. Therefore, in practice, the needs of power could not be fully justified in Buddhist terms. Amid the ruthless power practices of rulers, the Bodhisattva ideal proved an insufficient ideology for the state: even in Theravada Buddhist Burma, kingship remained based on Hindu concepts. Hinduism's relativistic ethics provided more effective principles for the *pragma* of power than could the Buddhist ethos of overcoming universal suffering: "Forgiveness shown to friend or foe is an ornament in the case of hermits, while the same shown to offenders by kings is a blemish," says a Hindu maxim influential among Burmese rulers.

It was through a "withering away" of the state that Buddhist social ideals were expected to find ultimate fulfillment: in a previous life, the subsequent Buddha's message had induced the king and a multitude of his subjects to abandon the kingdom and to become monks in the forest. Invaders who overran the country to seize its treasures had joined with the subsequent Buddha and the king in renouncing power and wealth. The latter "caused . . . his treasury to be thrown open, [so that] his treasures . . . would be exposed . . . that all who pleased might take of them." The ideal Buddhist world ruler of the future, the Cakkavatti Samkha, will renounce status and distribute his wealth to the poor, the homeless, and the destitute, and he himself will wander in homelessness. He and his army, and the enormous crowds accompanying them, will become monks: the Cakkavatti will usher in the age of Mettaya, the future Buddha. Yet self-identification with the Cakkavatti by the Burmese conqueror Bodawpaya (1782-1819) may have contributed to Burma's westward expansion that ended in the First Anglo-Burmese War (1824-26). At a time when territorial losses and indemnity payments were putting a considerable burden upon the Burmese peasantry, there was first recorded a popularization of the canonic Pali Cakkavatti prophecies, which have become the basis of the present-day Burma folklore about Setkya Min Buddha Yaza ("Lord of the Weapon and Buddha-Ruler"): when the reversion of the ethical and social order shall have reached its deepest point, he is to restore the observances of the Buddhist dharma, so that "the totality of Burma's people shall be made happy through an abundance of gold and silver and gems. [And the] people of the entire world shall equally become Buddhist [in religion]." All countries in the world are then to be ordered according to the Dharma Law.

In 1839, 1855, 1858, and 1860, peasants revolted, in the name of Setkya Min, against Burmese kings and British conquerors. Around Setkya Min pretenders centered Burmese guerrilla resistance against the British conquest in 1886-89, the attempted peasant rising of 1922, and particularly Saya San's peasant war of 1930-31. Saya San was executed, but his estate went to finance popularizations of Marxist literature in Burma. For though this nativistic reaction against the overwhelming impact of an alien civilization developed in a militant folk-Buddhist and animistic context, it overlapped with modernistic Burmese revolutionary nationalism, which also grew out of the disintegration of Burma's Buddhist society under British colonial rule.

British rule abandoned the state sponsorship of Buddhism in the name of liberalism but under the influence of Victorian missionary Protestantism. Thus the missionary-scholar Spence Hardy argued that such "nations have been placed under our authority, that we might carry on with better effect . . . the world's conversion from darkness to light and from the power of Satan unto God."[4] Against such attacks, the lay Buddhism of the English-educated Burmese invoked the testimony of Western critics of historical Christianity: the beginning of the twentieth century was, in Europe, a time of disappointment in modern civilization, progress, and Christendom, a time when Europe developed self-doubts about her civilization and her mission. Theo-

sophic idealizations of Indic religion, Nietzschean attacks on
Christian beliefs, the social gospel's challenge to orthodoxy,
and Marxist attacks on the economics of empire-building, all
stimulated the apologetics of a modernist Buddhism. Among
the Englishmen converted to Buddhism was Gordon Douglas,
"son of a well-known Earl . . . , said to have come to the East
. . . owing to his being an out and out radical with socialistic
tendencies"![5] As a Buddhist monk, under the name "Bhikkhu Ashoka," he died in 1900 in Bassein, in southern Burma.

Modernist Buddhism began to shift the traditional quest
for deliverance from cosmic suffering into the direction of a
quest for deliverance from social suffering. The Ceylonese
Dharmapala, its main spokesman, talked by 1913 about
"Buddha's social gospel." Claims that the peoples of Indic
civilization had yet to be trained for self-government came to
meet militant rejection, first in terms of liberal slogans of
self-determination borrowed from the West, and subsequently in the form of re-interpretations of old Indic culture
as containing indigenous democratic traditions. After the
British capture of Burma's last king, Buddhist modernists
transferred the monastic community's republican principles
to the realm of political ideology.

As tradition had attributed to the omniscient Buddha "all
the remedies that are current in the world for the benefit and
welfare of man, . . . all the expedients for the service of
man," so the revolutionary watchwords of fraternity, equality, and social justice came to be attributed to the Buddha
under the pressure of twentieth-century conditions. Thus the
thesis of a "Buddhist socialism" antedates World War I.
Lakshmi Narasu's *The Essence of Buddhism,* published in
1907, already expresses a Buddhist anti-capitalism whose
radical tone anticipates subsequent Communist slogans. A
considerable part of Burma's modernistic Buddhism became
associated with the independence movement. Its economic
demands had, in the Burmese cultural context, a Buddhist

justification. "To be able to give alms [to the nirvana-seeking monks], one must first make provisions for one's well-being before parting with what one has to give to another," wrote the abbot Zeyawadi U Thilasara, in 1923.[6]

Thereby the goal of a nirvana-within-life was endowed with revolutionary meaning. Sayadaw Zeyawadi U Thilasara described the stages of political struggle toward independence as parallel to the stages of Buddhist deliverance from the state of an ordinary human to final release by means of supreme Enlightenment. Independence for Burma was to mean nirvana-within-this-world, according to the poet Thakin Kudaw Hmain. Not only outward freedom but even ultimate liberation into nirvana was to be reached through the independence struggle, declared Sayadaw U Nye Ya, a popular preacher active in Burma's Buddhist revival. Most prominent among the political monks was U Ottama. He provided the modernist elite's aspirations for independence with roots in traditional folk Buddhism. The Buddhist populace could become the mass basis for political minority aspirations, once it was attracted by the "new" emphasis on *political* conditions for the pursuit of nirvana-within-this-world: this symbol reflected the folkloric memories of medieval Burmese state ideals and the popular prophecies about the perfect Buddhist society of the future.

According to Buddhist tradition, good government was expected to produce an ethical harmony in nature in which crops would grow without human labor. The government desired by the traditionalist majority of the Burmese was to be a cornucopia, an inexhaustible source of plenty: the ideal Buddhist state would assure that plenty as a prerequisite for leisure and meditation toward nirvana. Its arrival was to follow the Age of Decline—and decline seemed manifest in Buddhist Burma by the time of the Great Depression. Between 1870 and 1930, agricultural real wages in Lower Burma fell by an estimated 20 per cent. Burmese rice consumption apparently fell by nearly 25 per cent between 1921 and 1941. The Burmese had failed to benefit in proportion to the development of their country's economy. Buddhist social ethics were ill adapted to a business society. The Theravada Buddhist ethos has little place for such economic virtues as saving, planning, and investing; hence, in Burma, Buddhist values remained an obstacle to rational accumulation, investment, and profit. During the fall of rice prices in the Great Depression, many Burmese rice cultivators were dispossessed by foreclosure of mortgages. By 1933, the agriculturalists of Lower Burma had lost 40 per cent of their land to moneylenders.

Marxism entered Burmese politics in the early 1930's, through the Thakin group of the Dobama Asiayon Party, which was to produce the political leaders of postwar Burma. The mentor of the Thakins was Kudaw Hmain. By the late 1930's, he is said to have become "the real ideologist" of the Thakins, and his thought served as the basis of Burma's postwar Buddhist socialism. In his book *Thakin Tika*, published in 1938, he recalled that, according to the Digha Nikaya Buddhist scripture, men had elected their first ruler and then voluntarily taxed themselves to provide for him and to maintain law and government. A later Burmese Communist leader, Thakin Than Tun, referred to the same Buddhist tradition of the existence of a primitive communist utopia before the aberration of selfishness produced private property and the need for governments. Indeed, the Buddhist scriptural account of the origin of government coincided both with the basic ideas of the social contract theory of early liberalism and with Marxist notions that the rise of private property gave birth to the state.

Since the only philosophical terms in the Burmese language are designations for Buddhist concepts, Buddhist terminology was the only one available to expound Marxism in Burma, if Marxism was to be widely understood. Thus even the most orthodox Burmese theorist of Marxism-Leninism, Thakin Soe, used Buddhist terminology to explain the unfamiliar new ideology in terms of the familiar old religion. The Buddhist term for the cyclical generation and destruction of worlds was used to designate the eternal flux of matter in dialectical materialism. The words for "strike" (*thabeit hmauk*) and "strikers" (*thabeit hmauk-thu*) were borrowed from the traditional gesture made by Buddhist monks when they refused to accept alms (inverting their bowls as a protest against the giver). On the other hand, the term *lokka nibban*, the worldly nirvana, is allegedly of Marxist origin. The concept seems to have developed as an offshoot of secularizing trends in Burma's Buddhist modernism of the 1920's.

These interpretations of Buddhism met with some opposition by the 1930's. To counter these anti-socialist objections with Buddhist arguments, U Nu wrote—around 1935 or 1936—his essay *Kyan-to Buthamd*, in which he presented socialism as the consequence of a lay Buddhist ethos. The socialism of the Buddhist modernists emphasized that as greed, hate, and delusion cause suffering, so are they in turn caused by economic injustice: economic reform was needed to eliminate these aberrations. U Nu wrote that the capitalist concentration of wealth reduced the number of those economically capable of performing works of Buddhist piety; thus the impact of capitalism on Burma was responsible for the people's turning away from religion. He stressed that men must have economic security in order to be able to meditate about the impermanence of material things. As the struggle for self-preservation was eased by reforms, so Buddhist piety would increase. According to U Nu, social reforms, the elimination of economic injustice, and the enrichment of the poor were not ends in themselves: they were but economic means for the achievement of a Buddhist religious goal. The unofficial anthem of his old Thakin party, the "Red Dragon

Song," announced that the people would be freed from poverty *to enable them* to perform good deeds and to build monasteries. This revolutionary song recalled the "gold and silver rains" that were reputed to have fallen under the virtuous rulers of medieval Burma and predicted the approach of a comparable era of abundance and wealth.

The constitution adopted by Burma after the recovery of independence contains socialist features. The Land Nationalization Law of 1948 was advocated by U Nu on Buddhist grounds. He declared that property has only a functional place as a means for the pursuit of nirvana (through meditation). The class struggle had arisen only from the illusion that property had value in itself, and this illusion had caused bloodshed throughout history; its overcoming would usher in a perfect society. In 1949 and again in 1950, U Nu recalled that "when the world began" the material needs of all peoples were satisfied by nature without human effort, until greed moved men to take more than they needed; the introduction of private property had caused want and misery ever since. He presented socialism as the teaching that could bring humanity back to the blissful perfection of the past. This was a political application of the Agganna Sutta of the Buddhist canon.

Though democracy and socialism were adapted by Burma from Britain, they were accepted within the context of the Buddhist social ethos. In Burma, the degree of Anglicization, even of the elite, was never as great as in Ceylon or India. Political independence increased the dependence of Burma's politicians upon the traditionalist majority, for whom the unfamiliar abstractions of democracy and socialism were comprehensible only in the familiar Buddhist context. Thus Buddhism was bound to leave a deep imprint on the reception of these borrowed Western political concepts by the Burmese public. This produced syncretistic rationalizations among the acculturated elite. Thus, U Ba Yin, a former

Minister of Education, wrote that Marx must have "directly or indirectly been influenced . . . by Buddha."[7] Modernists claimed that the Buddhist message calls for a break with the alien business society's materialist values more radically than does any platform of social revolution. Marxism was viewed as providing an economic methodology for the advancement of Buddhist goals. In 1950, U Ba Swe, leader of the Burmese Socialist Party, called Marxism a "lower truth" that could facilitate the achievement of the Buddhist "higher truth," since "reflections" about Aging, Disease, and Death "cannot be clearly answered by the Marxist *abhidhamma*" (philosophy). To U Ba Swe, Marxism was to provide material satisfaction: "While at the present time men, being lost in concerns about nourishment, concerns about clothing, and concerns about shelter cannot meditate about the phenomena of impermanence . . . they cannot free themselves from the fact of Death. But having obtained satisfaction for the corporeal frame through material well-being, they shall be able to meditate over Aging, Disease, and the fact of Death."[8]

But the Burmese Communists were not content to have Marxism accepted merely as a method of liberation from economic suffering within the far more comprehensive Buddhist methodology of liberation from universal suffering, just as they refused to be content with the position of junior partner in the coalition government of the Anti-Fascist People's Freedom League (AFPFL). In vain did U Nu offer to step down in favor of the Communists *if* they could achieve a majority in free elections; in 1948, they started an insurrection against the government. A Communist victory would have transformed Marxism from an economic tool for the Buddhist quest into an ideology monopolizing power. Against this background, U Nu abandoned "Marxism" in 1958, that is, he explicitly rejected the Marxist *political and ideological* doctrines of proletarian dictatorship and materialism—doctrines that he had, in fact, never accepted, even in his "Marxist" period. But in rejecting "Marxism," U Nu and the AFPFL did not intend to repudiate their Marxist *economic* program. This became evident after the split in 1958 between the followers of U Nu and those of U Ba Swe and U Kyaw Nyein. The latter continued to be influenced by revisionist Marxism, although *politically* their program hardly differed from U Nu's socialist platform. When U Nu triumphed overwhelmingly in Burma's last free election, in 1960, it was largely because of the popular Buddhist emphasis of his socialism. (U Nu was popularly regarded as a future Buddha.)

In a pre-election speech on November 16, 1959, U Nu referred to the traditional ideal of the perfect Buddhist ruler. He reiterated that the acquisitive economy had developed out of that illusion of self which Buddhism strives to overcome. And he emphasized that acquisitive competition prevents a social order that would make meditation economically possible for all, thereby permitting universal liberation from impermanence and suffering. From what has been stated, it is clear that this was not a pragmatic improvisation, but a modernized political application of a Buddhist political ethos professed in the inscriptions of Burma's old kings and partly preserved in the popular folklore of the Burmese.

By contrast, the use made of Buddhist arguments by the leftist puritanical dictatorship of the Burmese Army, which overthrew U Nu in 1962, is truly pragmatic. An associate of the pro-Marxist Yahan Nge Aphwe monks' organization, the Buddhist monk Shin Okkahta, who had been accused of pro-Communist deviation from Buddhist teachings, is believed to have participated in formulating the program of Ne Win's Revolutionary Council. Its philosophic excursions use Buddhist causation terminology (*paticcasamuppada*) for dialectics. However, Buddhism is no longer a state religion under the military dictatorship, which is not disposed to be the patron of the monastic orders. Its approach is secular, although not necessarily anti-Buddhist: when Buddhist monks criticized the Revolutionary Council's rule as Communist, the Council emphasized that, unlike Communist governments, it permits its members to remain Buddhists. Though the Communists and their fronts were the only political groups to approve—at least initially—the usurpation of power by Ne Win, their attitude toward Buddhism is in practice far more negative than the Army's: the same Communist leader Thakin Soe who once started the practice of popularizing Marxist concepts in Buddhist terminology ordered Buddhist monks killed in the territories overrun by his "Red Flag" Communists (a militant "left" faction sometimes described as "Trotskyite").

Far less violent have been "Trotskyite" developments in Ceylon. There the "Viplavakari" offshoot of the "Trotskyite" Lanka Sama Samaj Party, led by Philip Gunawardena, included prominent Buddhist monks and advocated state sponsorship of the majority Buddhist religion. Having separated from the Bandaranaike government coalition, Gunawardena's group even joined one of the most communalistic Sinhalese organizations, the Association of the Moral Law (Dharma Samaj). However, Gunawardena did demand an investigation of the business activities of certain enterprising monks, one of whom—for personal business reasons—had organized the murder of Bandaranaike in 1959. In 1960, Bandaranaike's widow obtained a majority of seats in Parliament (though not of the popular vote) through electoral agreements with the Marxist parties. The fact that Catholics and other non-Buddhists led the anti-socialist military and police conspiracy of 1962 strengthened the Communist and Trotskyite appeal to Buddhist sentiment. In 1962, the main Marxist party, the Lanka Sama Samaj, re-entered the coalition government under Mme. Bandaranaike. Subsequently, most of the Buddhist monkhood turned against her coalition, mainly because of the government's taxation of monastery lands. As a result, the socialist Bandaranaike government was voted out of power in 1965, and Ceylon resumed a form of neutralism more favorable to free enterprise and to the West.

Cambodia

Political developments have been very different in Cambodia. Even as a protectorate of France (1863-1945), Cambodia succeeded in preserving its Buddhist kingship and traditional outlook. The independence of the country was restored by its ruler, Norodom Sihanouk, without the trauma of a revolutionary war of liberation. This was achieved externally by diplomatic skill and internally through a charisma that invokes Cambodia's medieval kingship. Norodom Sihanouk is fond of quoting Jayavarman VII (ca. 1200 A.D.), for whom "the pain of the subjects and not his own pain was the sadness of rulers; forever lasts his intercession among the charitable kings of Cambodia." After the Hindu god-kings had exhausted the resources of medieval Cambodia, that country's later rulers came to profess the Theravada Buddhist royal ethos of economic welfare for the people as a means to give them leisure to meditate and thus to reach salvation in nirvana. The survival of such a Buddhist charisma of kingship in the mind of the traditionalist majority of Cambodians permitted Norodom Sihanouk to renounce the throne in order to appeal to the masses on the level of party politics; and it was just this that enabled him to rule with enormous majorities of the popular vote that are unknown in free elections elsewhere. According to an official formulation of Norodom Sihanouk's political ideology, his "Cambodian socialism" is founded on Buddhism. The official ideological

platform of the Cambodian government explicitly interprets
Buddhism as "socialism"—in terms of the traditional striving
toward the overcoming of universal suffering. It is alleged
that ancient Cambodia practiced a form of socialism, without
giving it that name. But precisely this association of socialism
with the traditional national culture is used to answer the
Communists with the claim that it is unnecessary to force
revolution upon Cambodia, unlike the case of Communist
countries whose previous history had not given them a
socialism of their own.

This Buddhist-motivated welfare state program of Cambodia happens to correspond to the requirements of a planned
economy for an underdeveloped country lacking private
capital accumulation and native entrepreneurial classes. Because southern Buddhism has not sanctified acquisitiveness,
the vast majority of Cambodians are not accustomed to
thinking that much can be gained by owning more land than
one can work oneself. The accumulation of property is not
religiously sanctified and property in itself ensures neither
prestige nor the social respect that is bestowed upon the
search for self-perfection. On the other hand, the efforts for
economic emancipation and national security stimulate in
Cambodia, too, modernist re-interpretations of these Buddhist
social ethics (re-interpretations that have developed previously
in more Western acculturated Ceylon). The Cambodian
government also seeks to popularize the modernist idea that
the aspiration for material happiness in this earthly life is
Buddhist and has a positive value: by that the Cambodian
state attempts to counter the monopolization of acquisitive
middle-class roles by the Chinese and Vietnamese minorities.

The historical fear of Vietnam (of which only the South
borders on Cambodia) still determines Norodom Sihanouk's
stand in relation to the Communist and anti-Communist
powers. He has repeatedly denounced Communism as a
threat to Cambodia's Buddhist traditions. The main reason

for the anti-Americanism of this neutralist leader is the fact that his Vietnamese and Thai neighbors, who have been Cambodia's historical enemies, are now allies of the United States. Since 1963, public opinion in Cambodia has been further antagonized by the tribulations of the Vietnamese Buddhists in the anti-Communist South.

Notes

1. *Bulletin de l'Ecole-Française d'Extrême Orient*, XXXIII (1933), 650.
2. R. Spence Hardy, *The British Government and the Idolatry of Ceylon* (London, 1841), p. 6.
3. *Ibid.*, p. 7.
4. *Ibid.*, p. 6.
5. *Journal of the Maha-Bodhi Society*, IX, No. 1 (May, 1900), 3.
6. Zeyawadi U. Thilasara, article in *Pinnya Alin* of Waning-Wagaung, 1285 Burmese era (September 1, 1923).
7. Po Yarzar [U Ba Yin], "Letters to a Communist Nephew," Letter IV, in *The Burmese Review*, December 6, 1948.
8. U Ba Swe-i, *Bama to hlan yei: hnin lou'tha: lu: du* (Rangoon, 1955), p. 44.

V

SUN YAT-SENISM AS A MODEL FOR SYNCRETISTIC IDEOLOGIES OF DEVELOPING COUNTRIES

GOTTFRIED-KARL KINDERMANN

On November 12, 1966, the 100th anniversary of the birth of Sun Yat-sen the "Father of the Chinese Revolution," the "Founder of the Chinese Republic," and the "Prophet of China's Political Re-emergence," was commemorated both in Taiwan and in mainland China. To the Kuomintang regime, the creator of Chinese nationalism has remained the source of its official ideology and the object of a kind of state cult; but the Communists, too, still respect the founder of the Kuomintang as a great progressive figure, and indeed claim that they have fulfilled his testament after the Nationalists betrayed it. In the mid-1920's, Sun's revolutionary head-quarters at Canton had indeed become a temporary rallying point for Asian revolutionaries of the most divergent back-grounds, motives, and character. Chiang Kai-shek and Mao Tse-tung, Ho Chi Minh[1] and Chou En-lai, Wang Ching-wei as well as Hu Han-min, to mention only a few, had joined the camp of Sun Yat-sen during this brief period of revolutionary cooperation. All of them had been attracted and influenced in one way or another by the charismatic personality of this influential leader of China's national-revolutionary movement.

Western students have often been puzzled at the apparent discrepancy between the strength of the myth left behind by Sun Yat-sen and his seemingly limited achievements in the field of practical politics. Yet the true importance of the achievement was ideological—it lay in the pioneering effort to create a synthesis between the demands of progress and modernization on the one hand and the most vital elements of China's cultural tradition on the other. That synthesis not only became the first Chinese political philosophy to inspire the creation of a modern structure of political and military power;[2] it also developed a number of features and patterns that have since been repeated in the ideologies of other nationalist movements in Asia and Africa. In this study we shall briefly outline and analyze those features of Sunyatsenism that have proved of paradigmatic importance for other developing countries.

Ideological Voluntarism

As predicted by Karl Marx on the occasion of the Second Anglo-Chinese War, the Chinese revolution has largely assumed the form of a series of eruptive indigenous responses to the overpowering challenges from the West. The Western impact upon China had resulted not only in the destruction of China's traditional order and national independence, but also in the collapse of China's traditional self-image and world view. The self-styled "Middle Kingdom" found itself suddenly reduced to the status of a semicolonial area at the periphery of world affairs. Consequently, any practical adjustment to the new historical situation had to be preceded, or at least accompanied, by a readjustment of China's world view and by self-reappraisal. Hence, all the great political movements of modern China, from the

T'ung-Chih era to the Communist, have, with ever increasing radicalism, tried to achieve this readjustment to the realities and necessities of the modern world.

Sun Yat-sen's awareness that his movement was revolutionary, not only in its intended method of coming to power but also in its program for China's future, is clearly reflected in the founding manifesto of the Chinese Revolutionary League (Chung-kuo ko-ming t'ung-meng-hui) that he established in exile in Tokyo in 1905. The manifesto reads in part:

> The revolutions in former generations, such as the Ming Dynasty and the Taiping Heavenly Kingdom, were concerned only with the driving out of barbarians and the restoration of Chinese rule. Aside from these they sought no other change. We today are different from people of former times. Besides the driving out of the barbarian [Ch'ing] dynasty and the restoration of China, it is necessary also to change the national polity and the people's livelihood.[3]

Following the overthrow of the corrupt Ch'ing Dynasty, which kept itself ethnically segregated from the other component parts of the Chinese empire, China was to become a republic, the Chinese people were to rule themselves through a parliamentary form of government, land was to be redistributed to the farmers in a legal and evolutionary manner, and China's industrialization was to be preceded by the introduction of social legislation intended to prevent in China the social sufferings that had resulted from Europe's industrial revolution.

In the early phases of his political career, Sun seems to have been less convinced of the necessity of creating a cohesive body of ideological doctrines than he became later—after the more idealistic revolutionaries had, in the early years of the Republic, suffered repeated defeats at the hands of rival politicians who were more adept and more ruthless in the manipulation of political power. By the early 1920's, however, when his party was still far from seizing power in China, Sun was fully persuaded of the necessity to recast his political ideas into the mold of a cohesive doctrine that was to become his political legacy to his party and his people. In contrast to Mao Tse-tung who, after early failures, based the formulation of his ideological programs for the period preceding the Communist seizure of power in China upon crude—but effective—sociological and, especially, public opinion "surveys," Sun Yat-sen was more inclined to trust his intuition. Convinced of the necessity of a revolutionary ideology and of the correctness of his own concepts, he regarded his doctrine both as a means to inspire confidence, determination, and enthusiasm among his followers and as a definition of the goals that must be achieved if China's salvation and her restoration as an equal member in the family of nations were to be accomplished. Highly characteristic of this attitude are the opening sentences of Sun Yat-sen's principal ideological work, *San Min Chu I (The Three Principles of the People):*

> I have come here today to speak to you about the San Min Principles. What are the San Min Principles? They are, by the simplest definition, the principles for our nation's salvation. What is a principle? It is an idea, a faith, and a power. When men begin to penetrate into the heart of a problem, an *idea* generally develops first: as the idea becomes clearer, a *faith* arises; and out of the faith a *power* is born. . . . Why do we say that the San Min Principles will save our nation? Because they will elevate China to an equal position among nations, in international affairs, in government, and in economic life, so that she can permanently exist in the world. The San Min Principles are the principles for our nation's salvation.[4]

In similar fashion, Indonesian President Sukarno, addressing a Preparatory Committee for Independence (of Indonesia) on June 1, 1945, raised the question, "What is to be our *Weltanschauung* if we intend to establish an independent Indonesia?" The observation that most of the great political movements of the modern world had been based upon a body of political ideals and goals became for Sukarno the starting point for that question, and for his subsequent endeavor to develop such a *Weltanschauung* in the form of his Pantja Sila ideology.[5] As the former Indonesian Minister of Information, Ruslan Abdulgani, a close collaborator of Sukarno, told this author in 1963, Sukarno tended to consider himself in this respect as the "Sun Yat-sen of Indonesia."[6]

The central question—"What is to be our world view and self-image?"—is not confined to individual political leaders such as Sun Yat-sen and Sukarno. It is one of the key questions facing political movements and leaders in the new states, and indeed in all countries where a radical break with the past and the construction of a new political and social order are intended. The question is an expression of the search for a new sense of national identity that will correspond to the historic characteristics and the present needs of the country concerned, as well as to the political and economic realities of an increasingly interdependent modern world. Many of these ideological systems are voluntaristic, in the sense that they are not the outcome of a continuous evolution of political-philosophical thought but are rather the results of an ad hoc decision to create a new political philosophy, because the need for some systematic ideological motivation and orientation for political action is felt acutely. Sun Yat-sen happened to be one of the first Asian statesmen to feel this need and to respond to it by formulating his *San Min Chu I* ideology.

The Role of Cultural Tradition

On the basis of their attitude toward the indigenous cultural tradition of their respective countries, the ideological movements arising in Asian developing countries have been divided into three broad categories. The first group exhibits a *cultural iconoclasm,* which regards the total rejection and negation of the basic traditions of their countries' cultural heritage as a decisive prerequisite for the effective construction of a new social and political order based on a radically modernistic world view. The secularist republicanism of the Kemalist movement in Turkey, the radical wing of China's May 4th Movement, and the Maoist line of Chinese Communism are characteristic examples of this type of cultural iconoclasm.

A second group of ideologies may be regarded as *traditionalist* because they proclaim their intent to preserve and defend as much as possible of their countries' traditional cultural values and institutions against the encroachments of what is often called the "cultural imperialism of the West." The adherents of this type of ideology are above all to be found among orthodox and often fanatic religious groups, such as certain extremist Hindu movements in India or the Moslem Brotherhood in Egypt. Mohandas K. Gandhi expressed something of this spirit when he said:

> It is a charge against India that her people are so uncivilized, ignorant, and stolid that it is not possible to induce them to any changes. It is a charge really against our merit. What we have tested and found true on the anvil of experience we dare not change. Many thrust their advice upon India, and she remains steady. This is her duty; it is the sheet anchor of our hope.... And where this cursed modern civilization has not reached, India remains as it was before.... Now you see what I consider to be real civilization. Those who want to change conditions such as I have described are enemies of the country and are sinners.[7]

The largest group of development ideologies, however, is *syncretistic* in its endeavor to combine, in one way or another, certain basic values of the traditional cultural heritage with selected ideas and institutions copied from the West. This is the intention with which Sun Yat-sen has constructed his *San Min Chu I* ideology, and his example has been followed by the majority of contemporary founders of ideological systems in Asia and Africa. The basic aim of such syncretism is quite clear. Motivated by the fear of a loss of cultural identity, as well as by the desire for effective modernization, it seeks to preserve the one while simultaneously achieving the other. For reasons of national prestige or partial conviction, or both, syncretistic thinkers tend to stress the superiority of their own cultural tradition to that of the West, at least in certain spheres. Yet, at the same time, they proclaim their intention to learn from the latter's material achievements. This double-sided attitude creates a certain ambivalence. The classical syncretistic device for overcoming this ambivalence lies in the assertion that the predominant traditional force within their own culture—be it Confucianism, Hinduism, Buddhism, or Islam—has developed, earlier and better than Western civilization, certain basic ethical concepts whose validity is presently accepted by a majority of modern philosophies in East and West.

Sun Yat-sen, for example, was proud to claim that classical Confucianism had, five hundred years B.C., formulated the essential ideas of ethical humanism without reference to religious revelation, including such concepts as the primacy of love toward one's fellow men, the "golden mean," the character of rule by men over men as a trust (the "mandate of heaven"), and the right of rebellion against unethical rule. Sukarno has declared in his writings, as well as in the course of a conversation with this author, that he is a socialist *because* he is a Moslem. Long before, Hadji A. Salim, a leader of the Indonesian Sarekat Islam movement, had claimed that "the prophet (Muhammad) is the father of socialism and a guide toward democracy." And U Ba Yin, a prominent Burmese statesman, has argued that Buddhism, which teaches that men must achieve their salvation essentially on their own, is more democratic and more rational than the Christian idea of the "dictatorship of God."[8]

Yet, this method of extolling the values and achievements of the cultural past confronts syncretistic thinkers with another dilemma. It lies in the need for breaking down traditional political, social, and economic structures for the sake of modernization on the one hand, while seeking to uphold the central values of the cultural tradition on the other. Here again, Sun Yat-sen chose a solution that was later to be imitated by other ideologists of contemporary Asia. Sun's solution is to be found in his claim that the glories of classical Confucianism had been perverted and distorted by the epigones in subsequent phases and centuries of China's history; so the degenerated *ancien régime* had to be destroyed, among other reasons, in order to restore the time-transcending glory and effectiveness of authentic classical Confucian thought.

This method of introducing new concepts through a new interpretation of accepted philosophical traditions and systems is, of course, a familiar device in the history of Chinese philosophy. But Sun Yat-sen used this device for the solution of a new and vital problem faced by the majority of "developing countries" in our time. He found in it the formula that permitted him to attack the existing political order not only in the name of the necessity of China's adjustment to the modern world, but also in the name of those lasting ethical values of classical Confucianism whose preservation was to prevent the loss of China's cultural identity by a total capitulation before the cultural values and intellectual systems of the West.

Nationalism, Anti-Imperialism, and Pan-Asianism

Sun Yat-sen's *San Min Chu I* doctrine contains three basic pillars that have since reappeared as the cornerstones of the great majority of modern ideologies in contemporary Asia and Africa. Roughly translated, these are nationalism, democracy, and socialism. By preaching the principle of nationalism, Sun Yat-sen intended to create a new focus of political loyalty that could take the place of the traditional loyalty toward the ruling dynasty. This search for a central political idea that would be potent enough to overcome both the horizontal (regional) and vertical (social) divisions of Chinese society, caused Sun—and other political thinkers in developing countries—to put the strongest possible emphasis upon the dangers threatening China from foreign powers.

True enough, at the beginning of his revolutionary career, Sun, like other revolutionaries, optimistically assumed that the advanced industrial powers would necessarily sympathize with his revolutionary movement because of its modernizing intentions. Yet it is wrong to say that Sun's later anti-imperialism was merely the result of his having been influenced by Lenin's theories of imperialism. When, hardly one year after the victory of the Republican revolution of 1911-12, President Yüan Shik-k'ai began to suppress the newly established parliament, Sun Yat-sen, in the name of Chinese democracy, appealed to various foreign powers to desist from granting a substantial loan to the government of Yüan Shih-k'ai—but in vain. The London *Times* expressed the typical reaction of the Western press when it condemned "the wild and impractical dreams of the Young China Party." Only a few weeks later, the disappointment of the "dreamer" Sun, now back in exile, manifested itself in his first unequivocally anti-imperialist utterance: "Not our own people, not our own mistakes drove us from China, but foreign money power, deliberately employed for the break-up of our country."[9] Three years later, during the nation-wide debate over the question of China's entry into World War I, Sun wrote that "those who . . . advocate China's entry into the war, must be labouring under the delusion that China will gain benefits and honours from an Allied victory. They do not realize that China, with Russia at her back, will suffer a worse fate in case of an Allied victory than in case of an Allied defeat. Whether the Allies will win or not, China will be Britain's victim." And at the end of World War I, when Japan moved to seize Germany's former rights in Shantung province, Sun explained: "Japanese militarists, aiming at imperialism and forgetting the deeds and aspirations of the reformists, are trying to extend their aggressive policy to China, where they expect the least resistance."[10]

Thus, although Leninism has had a stimulating influence upon the formulation of Sun Yat-sen's anti-imperialism, it was not its original source; nor can it be said that Sun adopted all of Leninism's basic assumptions. He did not accept the Leninist vision of a "vertical" world revolution, in the sense of a global conflict between social classes, but he did believe in a "horizontal" type of world revolution—an uprising of the world's oppressed nations against the imperialist powers.[11] In Sun's view, the bulk of the oppressed nations were to be found in the colonial and semicolonial areas of the underdeveloped continents. However, he also included Bolshevik Russia after the Allied intervention and republican Germany after Versailles among the oppressed nations. This notion made it easy for him to form an alliance with Soviet Russia. And when Chiang Kai-shek—two years after the death of Sun Yat-sen—decided to terminate this first Sino-Soviet alliance, he explained, with arguments that were later to be repeated by his adversary Mao Tse-tung, that China's relations with Russia had to change because the Russian leaders had ceased to be genuine revolutionaries and had transformed their country into a new type of imperialist power.[12]

The slogan of Afro-Asian solidarity, formulated in the era of decolonization following World War II, thus had one of its forerunners in Sun Yat-sen's type of Pan-Asianism, which claimed that since the greatest number of oppressed nations were to be found in Asia, the liberation of Asia was practically tantamount to the liberation of the oppressed part of mankind. Sun's conclusion for China's future policy was summed up in the words: "China is potentially equal to ten Powers. . . . When China becomes strong again it will be our duty to help these [oppressed Asian nations] win back their freedom. . . . We should . . . look forward to the day when we shall become leaders in world reconstruction upon lines of international justice and good will."[13] It follows that the vision of a revolutionary liberation movement, composed of the oppressed developing countries of Asia, led by China, and directed against colonial imperialism is not in itself an invention of contemporary Maoism. A decisive difference emerges, however, if one compares the values underlying the concepts of Mao on one side and those of Sun Yat-sen on the other. While Mao uses a Marxist ideology that had originated as a synthesis of powerful trends of philosophic and economic thought in nineteenth-century Europe, even though in a form that has been modified by adaptations to the twentieth-century pressures of revolutionary and post-revolutionary Russia and China, Sun Yat-sen, like other syncretistic political thinkers of modern Asia after him, seeks to base his movement on the moral superiority of Asian cultures over the power-centered and materialistic motivations of Western thought.

The Kemalist Model in the Relations Between Soviet Russia and Chinese Nationalism

Like so many later statesmen in developing countries, Sun Yat-sen intended to cooperate with Russia in a manner that would secure a maximum of material and technical Soviet aid combined with a minimum of Russian or Chinese Communist interference in the internal affairs of the Nationalist revolutionary movement. The model of this type of arrangement of an alliance between a politically autonomous, ideologically non-Marxist and partly even anti-Marxist Asian national revolutionary movement with Soviet Russia and the Third International—was the relationship between early Kemalist Turkey and Soviet Russia. It was probably with this "Kemalist model" in mind that Sun drafted the famous Sun-Joffe agreement of 1923,[14] which preceded the development of organized cooperation between Soviet Russia and the Kuomintang. The Soviet delegate stated his agreement with Sun Yat-sen's view that "the Communist order or even the Soviet system cannot actually be introduced into China, because there do not exist here the conditions for the successful establishment of either Communism or Sovietism." In his conversations with Comintern delegate V. Dalin, Sun Yat-sen flatly refused to accept the Communist Party of China as a coalition partner of the Kuomintang and insisted upon a form of cooperation under which the Communist Party of China was reduced to the status of a peripheral organization supporting the Kuomintang, with leading Communists being permitted to join the Kuomintang as individuals. Through their acceptance of this arrangement, those Communist leaders formally placed themselves under the disciplinary authority of the Kuomintang. Sun Yat-sen, on his part, left no one in doubt about his opinion that Soviet Russia's unofficial alliance with the Chinese revolution was an alliance with and through the Kuomintang, and not the Communist Party of China.[15] It is hardly surprising that G. Maring (Sneevliet), acting on behalf of the Communist International, had difficulty in forcing this form of cooperation down the throats of the leaders of the Communist Party of China.

Despite his explicit rejection of the Marxist class war doctrine, and of its Leninist application in the era of "war Communism,"[16] Sun Yat-sen found an ideological basis (or rationalization) for his political cooperation with Russia in two main points: the first was, of course, the common hostility of Communist Russia and Nationalist China to those imperialist powers that both opposed revolutionary Russia and simultaneously denied to China and other Asian nations a position of equality in the family of nations. The second point was the similarity of the ultimate, social-utopian visions of a future classless and stateless world community in Confucian and Communist doctrine: Sun was fond of stressing that Sun Yat-senist socialism and Soviet socialism advocated different methods but shared the same final goal.

In recent years, other revolutionary nationalist leaders have succeeded in obtaining Soviet support on similar terms. As late as 1963, quite a number of Indonesian politicians told this author, for example, that the internal political constellation of Indonesia, with a powerful nationalistic army on the one side, an equally powerful Communist Party organization on the other, and a political leader at the center whose charisma was capable of holding together these contradictory forces, resembled to an astonishing degree the situation of the united front era in China two years preceding the death of Sun Yat-sen. In China, this united front ended with the liquidation of the Shanghai Commune by the forces of Chiang Kai-shek, in 1927. It ended in Indonesia with the failure of a Communist *coup d'état* in 1965, which was followed by the slaughter of tens of thousands of pro-Maoist Indonesian Communists. Yet, probably in order to prevent that important country from drifting completely into the camp of the Western powers, the Soviet Union has continued its diplomatic recognition and economic support of post-Sukarno Indonesia.

After years of siding with the Soviets in most international questions in return for economic and military aid, while refusing to tolerate a legal Communist Party in competition with their official state parties, both Ben Bella in Algeria and Nasser in Egypt finally obtained, in 1963-64, a Soviet directive to the local Communists to join those state parties, and that directive has outlasted not only the reign of Khrushchev but also that of Ben Bella (despite the severe temporary setback the Algerian Communists suffered at his fall). After the Middle Eastern crisis of the summer of 1967, Soviet and Communist support for both Nasser and Boumedienne appears to be more firmly pledged than ever. In Burma, too, the Soviets seem to have accepted General Ne Win's claim of a political monopoly for his state party; but in view of the competition from Peking, Soviet influence on the Burmese Communists would hardly appear sufficient to implement the agreement. At any rate, Sun Yat-sen's interpretation of the Kemalist model of cooperation with Moscow has had a remarkable revival among the Afro-Asian nationalists of our time.

Democracy and Tutelary Dictatorship

There is another political dilemma for which the experience of Sun Yat-sen and his movement, and the type of solution found by him, have assumed paradigmatic importance for many other developing countries in Asia and Africa. The origin of this dilemma lies in each case in a failure of the attempt to introduce an effective system of democratic government. About one year after the victory of the Chinese Revolution, Sun Yat-sen and his adherents were driven from their country by Marshal Yüan Shih-k'ai, who established a military dictatorship. Convinced by this experience that a democratic system of government could not be introduced in China by a mere act of will of a revolutionary elite, Sun Yat-sen accepted the necessity of a period of revolutionary party dictatorship; but as he was determined to hold on to the democratic ideal as one of the cornerstones of his "Three Principles of the People," his solution was to introduce the idea of a "tutelary party dictatorship." The function of this tutelary dictatorship was to ensure the stability and integrity of government for the transitional period between the seizure of power by the revolutionaries and the time when conditions would be ripe for the introduction of an effective system of representative democracy. It was a solution that permitted both the exercise of party dictatorship in practice, and also, without logical contradiction, the continued upholding of democracy as an ideological principle and future goal to be realized by the revolutionary party.

To explain this tutelary system of government, Sun compared the function of his party in relation to the Chinese people during this transitional phase with the role of a scholarly statesman, in the days of imperial China, who had to prepare a youthful and still immature emperor for his future tasks of government. In the Chinese Republic, he explained, the sovereign was not an emperor but the Chinese people as a whole. Since the early years of the republic had demonstrated that the sovereign people, having been accustomed to autocratic rule for thousands of years, were not as yet sufficiently prepared for democratic government, the revolutionary party had the task of educating the new sovereign in the practice of self-government.[17] During this period of tutelary government by the party, the latter's dictatorship could be justified by its objective of facilitating its own replacement by effective representative institutions after a limited number of years. In the following "constitutional era," the mistake of simply copying constitutional patterns from Western nations was not to be repeated. China was to have a syncretistic "five-power constitution," combining the three powers of the Western liberal tradition (executive, legislative, judiciary) with two additional powers rooted in the traditions of pre-modern Chinese government: the power of control, derived from the censorial system of imperial China, and the examining power, which was to restore the tradition of selecting public office-holders through competitive examinations.[18]

The problems thus attacked in Sun Yat-sen's theory of government have reappeared with varying solutions in the political thought of other developing countries. Briefly summarized, they are, first, the problem of combining (after early unsatisfactory experiments with parliamentary government) the practice of dictatorship with the upholding of the ideal of democracy; and, second, the problem of creating a modern constitution not by simply copying Western models but by utilizing essentially indigenous institutions in modernized form.

In Indonesia, Sukarno found a theoretical solution for both of these problems by proclaiming the principle of "guided democracy" (the achievement of unanimity among representatives through intensive discussions under the guidance of the leader, a method derived from certain traditions of Indonesian village democracy), and by re-introducing the Indonesian constitution of 1945, which strengthened the position of the president. In the *Political Manifesto,* his most important ideological writing, Sukarno commented on both measures:

> Yes, indeed, without concealing anything we have made a complete divorce from Western democracy, which is free-fight liberalism, but on the other hand since ancient times we have flatly rejected dictatorships. Guided democracy is the democracy of the family system, without the anarchy of liberalism, without the autocracy of a dictatorship. Who for instance would say that Sun Yat-sen was a dictator, except maybe those kinds of imperialists who attack us? In one of his speeches Sun Yat-sen once said: "The greatest obstacle to democracy came from those who advocated unrestricted political democracy, but also from those who did no longer dare to advocate democracy."

Similarly, Pakistan President Ayub Khan complained that the British parliamentary system that his country had inherited and adopted in its constitution of 1956 "takes for granted too many prerequisites which do not really exist in a country like Pakistan." But, at the same time, he asserted that the *coup d'état* of 1958 was "not aimed against the institution of democracy as such" but was only directed "against the manner in which its institutions were being worked." The Mohammedan traditions of "equality" and "fraternity" can be used, according to Ayub Khan, as cornerstones of a democratic system for a modern Islamic state. After categorically stating the compatibility of Islam with modern democracy, Ayub Khan then raises the decisive question, "What type of democracy?" Since foreign models did not offer any viable solution, the new Pakistan constitution was to be shaped according to the needs and conditions of the country. This new constitutional system, according to Ayub Khan, was to function in such a way that each voter would be required to respond only to such questions "as he can answer in the light of his own personal knowledge and understanding without external prompting." After a brief transitional period of dictatorship, in which he acted as the "Administrator" of the country, Ayub Khan introduced his system of "basic democracy." It consists of a pyramidal structure of local and regional representative bodies: the chairmen of the councils elected at the lowest level of this pyramid form the councils at the next higher and geographically broader level, and so on to the top.[19]

In the United Arab Republic, President Nasser condemned the type of parliamentary government that had existed in Egypt between 1923 and 1952 as a "formal" democracy that actually served only the interests of a privileged oligarchy. Nasser admitted that the presidential system of one-party government that he introduced in 1956 was only a "transitional" solution. The transitional system, however, would provide "the basis for a full democracy, and then new political forces shall emerge. Then there may be groups, blocs, parties and even an opposition. I myself would welcome such a development." Again we have here the "tutelary" self-image of a national revolutionary elite that describes its dictatorial rule as a transition on the road to some higher stage of democracy. A plan for an evolution of self-government in stages, resembling Sun Yat-sen's ideas, starting from the bottom (local government) and moving to the top (the national state), is indeed outlined in the Charter of the United Arab Republic.[20]

Other cases of combining democratic ideals with the practice and justification of dictatorship in the ideologies of developing countries in Asia and Africa could be cited.[21] All of them reflect the same two basic facts: on the one hand, the search for forms of government that will prove suitable to the real sociological structures, development levels, and cultural traditions of the countries concerned and, on the other, the recognition of the need to pay at least verbal tribute to the ideal of democracy. While the prospects for the realization of this ideal may not be very promising in the majority of cases, the example of Turkey has demonstrated that the self-transformation of a development-dictatorship into a democratic multiparty system is possible: it need not be a mere deception, or self-deception, of those who promise it in the future while remaining in possession of dictatorial power.

Pragmatic Socialism and International Aid

A further programmatic trend shared by the great majority of development ideologies centers around the slogan of "socialism." Years before the October Revolution in Russia, Sun Yat-sen had expounded the theory that a form of socialism should and could be introduced at a moment when China's capitalism had not yet been fully developed. It would be possible in China to counteract the social evils produced by early capitalism in Europe if the revolutionary party would learn from the European experience. In practice, Sun intended to create in China a system of social and economic legislation that would prevent China's growing capitalism from becoming socially destructive.

In a famous article, written in July, 1912, Lenin criticized Sun Yat-sen for having displayed an "inimitable, one might say, virgin naiveté" in his "reactionary Narodnik theory" planning to anticipate and to forestall the negative effects of nascent capitalism in China.[22] Lenin's charge that the "subjective socialism" of Sun Yat-sen committed a reactionary mistake in hoping to avoid capitalism by a planned leap from "feudalism" to socialism had its ideological roots in the earlier Marxist polemic against the similar hopes of the Russian Narodniki.

Only three years after the Bolshevik Revolution, however, Lenin sharply reversed the position he had taken in his critique of Sun Yat-senist voluntarism. Speaking at the Second Congress of the Communist International, in 1920, Lenin declared that in certain conditions, the backward "pre-capitalist" nations would be able to "pass to the Soviet system and, after passing through a definite stage of development, to Communism, without passing through the capitalist stage of development."[23] The basis for this contention rested upon the experience of Russian-guided, "socialist" economic development in the Soviet-controlled backward areas of the former Russian empire, and on the expectation that the victorious proletariat of the most advanced countries would soon be able to offer the former colonies similar aid.

The economic program of Sun Yat-sen envisaged the nationalization of basic industries and means of communication, vigilant government supervision and legislative limitation of free enterprise, and a legal land reform, to be carried out by nonviolent methods, aimed at implementing his famous slogan "Land to the Tiller." Sun Yat-sen set another example for the nationalist ideologies of many developing countries when his closer contact with Soviet Russia caused him to stress the need for the revolutionaries to rely on the support of the workers and peasants, while strictly rejecting any idea of advocating class war within China. His argument was that the working classes of China were being exploited by foreign rather than by nascent Chinese capitalism, and that the Chinese capitalists themselves were suffering under the yoke of foreign economic imperialism. As a land reform that would arouse the least opposition from the millions of Chinese landlords, Sun Yat-sen advocated the nationalization of the unearned increment in land value, a method that had been carried out successfully in the former German-leased territory of Kiaochow in Shantung province.[24]

To be effective, however, this method required a rapid increase in land values, which would have to be brought about by intensive economic development. This may have been one reason why Sun Yat-sen conceived his well-known plan for the "international development of China."[25] First presented to the public immediately after the end of World War I, this bold project proposed a joint effort by several industrial powers, under the politically neutral supervision of the League of Nations, to give massive development aid to China.

Sun strongly emphasized that for a country like China, living on the verge of starvation, there were only two basic methods of development. The first was to accumulate capital through an intensified export of agricultural commodities, a method that was likely to entail considerable sufferings for the Chinese population. The alternative method, which Sun himself preferred, was to obtain substantial foreign loans. To prevent the power of the creditor nations from being politically abused to the disadvantage of China, Sun Yat-sen not only proposed a multinational effort by several industrial powers, but was moreover the first Asian statesman to suggest neutral administration of this aid by the League of Nations.

In Indonesia, Sukarno, in his ideological utterances, also refused to imitate any European pattern of socialism and insisted on introducing a "socialism à la Indonesia," which was to be "adjusted to conditions prevailing in Indonesia . . . to the people of Indonesia, to the customs, the psychology and culture of the Indonesian people." In this Indonesian socialism, "guided economy" was to be a corollary of "guided democracy." Sukarno defined the former by saying: "The economy shall be organized as a common endeavour based upon the principle of the family system. . . . Branches of production which are important for the State and which affect the life of most people shall be controlled by the State." Like Sun Yat-sen, Sukarno advocated a land reform that would expand land ownership (especially among the small farmers) and abolish the system of landlordism. He adopted Sun Yat-sen's slogan "Land to the Tiller," while at the same time explaining: "And yet, do not imagine that the land reform which we want to implement is 'Communist.' We still recognize the property rights over land." Sukarno gave a clear indication of his unwillingness to adopt Maoist methods in the execution of social reforms in Indonesia when he stated: "In Pantja Sila, the teaching does not hold that 'the aim of socialism justifies all means.' " The Pantja Sila principles would not permit the achievement of social reforms forced upon the people from above against their conviction by the dictatorial fiat of the ruling elite. All the groups and classes inside Indonesia who sincerely opposed colonialism and imperialism were invited to join the revolutionary movement. Contrary to Mao Tse-tung, and like Sun Yat-sen, Sukarno did not consider any group or class within the Indonesian population as an "objective enemy" that would have to be liquidated if genuine social progress were to be possible.

A similar rejection of Stalinist and Maoist methods of development is implied in the Charter of the United Arab Republic, which, after condemning capitalism and colonialism, speaks of "other experiments under extremely cruel pressure exercised on living generations, who were deprived of all the fruit of their labour for the sake of a promised future that they could not see or reach. Again, other peoples achieved their drive [toward reform] but after they had been subjected to inhibitions, terror and oppression. . . . The working class cannot be driven through forced labour to realize the objectives of production."[26] The proclaimed aim of the Egyptian land-reform legislation of 1952 and 1961 was to increase the number of owner-farmers. The nationalization of land was explicitly rejected, and the "individual ownership of land, within limits that would not allow for feudalism" was advocated.

With regard to foreign development aid, however, the Arab Charter goes beyond the argument of Sun Yat-sen, who tended to stress the mutual benefit of foreign aid to both recipient and donor. The Charter categorically states that "offering aid is the optional duty of the advanced states. It is a form of tax that must be paid by the states with a colonialist past to compensate those they exploited for so long."[27]

The natural tendency among developing countries to seek special forms of foreign development aid "without any political strings attached" expresses itself in contemporary international relations as well, but no longer primarily in terms of multinational aid-pooling under the supervision of the United Nations. Rather than cling to this pattern, which was first advanced by Sun Yat-sen, an increasing number of developing countries seek to achieve a de facto political neutralization of foreign development aid through the establishment of a more or less subtle balance of power between various rival donor nations. The maintenance of this type of balance has been effectively used as a weapon not only against attempts by donor nations to exercise political pressure through the medium of foreign aid, but occasionally also against the purely technical controls aimed at the most efficient employment of development aid by the recipient country.

Mao Tse-tung and the Myth of Sun Yat-sen

Any syncretistic ideology retains an element of ambiguity; hence the risk inherent in all political ideologies—that they may be used in future situations to justify conflicting policies—is particularly strong in the case of syncretistic philosophies. Sun Yat-senism has not escaped this risk. It may therefore be pertinent to conclude this brief survey with a discussion of the manner in which Mao Tse-tung utilized the myth of Sun Yat-sen in his ideological writings during the decade immediately preceding the final victory of the Chinese Communists. In fact, in those writings, notably, *On New Democracy* (January, 1940), *New Democratic Constitutionalism* (February, 1940), *On Coalition Government* (April, 1945), and *On People's Democratic Dictatorship* (June, 1949), no political authority, not excepting Marx, Lenin, and Stalin, is referred to more frequently in support of Mao's policies than is Sun Yat-sen.

Mao's use of the myth of Sun Yat-sen, especially during the years of simultaneous cooperation and conflict with the Nationalist government in the war against Japan, reflects both his awareness of the strength of the myth and his recognition that the propagation of purely Communist goals and doctrines would dangerously limit his party's appeal. Mao's famous theory of the "New Democratic Revolution" enabled him to concentrate his party's struggle during the "democratic phase" of the Chinese revolution—which was to precede and prepare the later "socialist phase"—on a "minimum program," and this, he claimed, amounted substantially to applying in practice Sun Yat-sen's "Three Principles of the People."

For example, after extensive "opinion surveys" had been carried out by Communist cadres in rural areas, Mao decided to adopt Sun Yat-sen's slogan "Land to the Tiller." In 1940, he wrote:

> The republic will adopt certain necessary measures to confiscate the land of landlords and distribute it to those peasants having no land or only a little land, carry out Dr. Sun Yat-sen's slogan of "land to the tillers," abolish the feudal relations in the rural areas, and turn the land into the private property of the peasants. In the rural areas, rich peasant economic activities will be tolerated. This is the line of "equalisation of land ownership." The correct slogan for this line is "land to the tillers." In this stage, socialist agriculture is in general not yet to be established.[28]

Few Chinese farmers indeed would have been attracted at that time by the idea of rural collectivization, or by the vision of having to work under the military discipline of a people's commune.

At the same time, in order to use Sun Yat-sen's authority as a means to dispel the fears of non-Communist Chinese that cooperation with the Communists might lead to a growth of Communist power, Mao resorted to the time-honored Chinese method of "re-interpreting" Sun Yat-senism. He referred to "the revolutionary, new, or genuine Three Principles of the People," claiming that Sun's policies of alliance with Soviet Russia, cooperation with the Chinese Communists, and assistance to the workers and peasants had become indispensable cornerstones of Sun's ideological system at the end of his life.[29] These "three great policies" *(San-ta cheng-ts'e)*—a term never used by Sun himself, but invented later by the Communists—were in fact advocated in the Political Manifesto of the First National Congress of the Kuomintang in January, 1924; Mao now argued that this manifesto contained Sun's own re-interpretation of his ideological system, and was indeed its last valid version.[30]

To the historian, this argument has obvious weaknesses. Though the manifesto was adopted in January, 1924, Sun actually laid down the final version of his Three Principles of the People in lectures delivered between January and August of that year. Yet in none of his other writings are Sun's criticism of the theory and practice of Soviet Communism and his recognition of Confucian values more explicit than in this final version—a fact all the more remarkable in that it was formulated at the height of Sun's practical cooperation with Soviet Russia and the Chinese Communists. As far as his party's relations with the Chinese Communists were concerned, Sun had, as we have seen, flatly refused to accept them as coalition partners of the Kuomintang, had forced their leaders to submit at least formally to the discipline of the Kuomintang, and had insisted that the Kuomintang and not the Chinese Communist Party was to be Moscow's partner in China.[31]

In his last will, Sun asked the members of his party "to join hands with those countries which are prepared to treat us as equals in our fight for the common cause of humanity," without, however, explicitly mentioning any particular country. In the last days of his life, he signed a letter addressed to the Central Committee of the Communist Party of the Soviet Union, in which he mentioned that he had asked the Kuomintang to be "in constant contact" with the CPSU and expressed his hope that one day "a mighty, free China" would cooperate with Soviet Russia in the liberation of the oppressed peoples of the world.[32] The Chinese Communists were, significantly enough, not mentioned in the letter. On the other hand, Sun had also stated in his last public speech, in Kobe, that "Japan and China must join hands and harmoniously lead the Asiatics to fight for Pan-Asianism, thus expediting world peace."[33]

It is thus difficult to accept Mao's claim that Sun Yat-sen's policy of cooperation with Soviet Russia is to be regarded as a keystone of Sun Yat-sen's ideological system. It is safe to say, however, that Sun's main condition for cooperating with *any* foreign power—be it Russia or Japan—was the recognition in word and deed of China's equality and her indisputable right to political self-determination. It is equally safe to assume that the precedent of Soviet Russia's relations with Turkey,[34] the wording of the Sun-Joffe joint statement of 1923, and the seeming submission of the Chinese Communist Party to the leadership of the Kuomintang had encouraged Sun in his hope that Soviet Russia would continue to support the Kuomintang's endeavor to build a new China based on the visions and plans of Sun Yat-sen.

Since the victory of the Communists on the Chinese mainland in 1949, and even more since their explicit transition from the "democratic" to the "socialist" phase of their revolution, Mao and his party have ceased to refer to the ideas of Sun Yat-sen as a justification and guidance for their present and future policies; yet they still recognize Sun's progressive role in Chinese history. The ambiguity of Sun Yat-senism has lent itself to conflicting interpretations, and the intended synthesis has been destroyed in the struggle. But this ambiguity has allowed widely divergent political forces to project their different concepts and goals onto the words of the teacher, and this has kept the attraction of the myth alive, far beyond the confines of China, wherever modernizing nationalists in developing countries are grappling with similar problems.

Significantly enough, the common veneration of Sun Yat-sen is the last ideological link bridging the deep chasm that presently divides the ruling forces in mainland China from those on Taiwan. Should changing circumstances on both sides allow a *rapprochement* of those forces on any future occasion, the cult of Sun Yat-sen might easily assume a new ideological function of integrating strength and historical importance.

Notes

1. Concerning Sun Yat-sen's influence on Ho Chi Minh, see Jean Lacouture, *Ho Chi Minh* (London, 1958), pp. 38 and 211. See also Hoang Van Chi, *From Colonialism to Communism* (New York, 1964), pp. 42-43.
2. See Gottfried-Karl Kindermann, *Konfuzianismus, Sunyatsenismus und Chinesischer Kommunismus: Dokumente zur Begründung und Selbstdarstellung des Chinesischen Nationalismus* (Freiburg im Breisgau, 1963), pp. 15-74.
3. Translated, in part, as Document 56 in Teng Ssu-yü and John K. Fairbank, *China's Response to the West: A Documentary Survey 1839-1923* (Cambridge, Mass., 1954).
4. Sun Yat-sen's first San Min Chu I lecture, January 27, 1924. English translation by Frank W. Price in *Sun Yat-sen, The Principle of Nationalism* (Taipei, 1953).
5. *The Indonesian Revolution: Basic Documents and the Idea of Guided Democracy* (Department of Information, Republic of Indonesia [Djakarta, 1960]), pp. 34-52.
6. After referring to his earlier conversion to cosmopolitanism, Sukarno said in his speech of June 1, 1945: "But in 1918, thanks be to God, there was another man who recalled me, and that was Dr. Sun Yat-sen. In his work *San Min Chu I,* or The Three People's Principles, I found a lesson which exposed the cosmopolitanism taught by A. Baars. Ever since then, nationalism has been implanted in my heart, through the influence of The Three People's Principles. Therefore, if the whole Chinese People consider Dr. Sun Yat-sen their preceptor, be sure that Bung Karno [Brother Sukarno] also, an Indonesian, with the utmost respect will feel grateful to Dr. Sun Yat-sen until he lies in the grave." *(Ibid.,* p. 42.)
7. Mohandas K. Gandhi, *Indian Home Rule* (Ahmedabad, 1946); reprinted, in part, in Paul E. Sigmund (ed.), *The Ideologies of the Developing Nations* (rev. ed.; New York, 1967), pp. 103-13.
8. U Ba Yin, Burma's former Minister of Education, has written in this connection: "If there is God whose will is supreme, then there can be no freedom for the human will.... Dictatorship—whether God's or Man's—is totalitarianism with all the seeds inherent in such a system. . . . Buddha clearly saw what a dictatorship was in essence, a tyranny, and by his denial of the existence of the Great Dictator he freed mankind from the bondage of all forms of dictatorship and killed the germs of human tyranny. Buddha gave to humanity its charter of equality and freedom from fear and laid foundations for the establishment of a real world-wide democracy." U Ba Yin, "Buddha's Way to Democracy," *The Burman,* April 12, 1954, p. 7; as quoted in Emanuel Sarkisyanz, *Buddhist Backgrounds of the Burmese Revolution* (The Hague, 1964).

9. *The New York Tribune,* June 7, 1914.
10. Sun's essays on international politics during World War I, as well as writings and comments on Sino-Japanese relations, have been collected in Sun Yat-sen, *The Vital Problem of China* (Taipei, 1953).
11. See Sun Yat-sen's first San Min Chu I lecture, delivered on January 27, 1924. Sun, *op. cit.*
12. Chiang Kai-shek, "Declaration to Kuomintang Members" (Shanghai, 1927), and "Manifesto to the People" (Shanghai, 1927).
13. See Sun Yat-sen's San Min Chu I lecture of March 2, 1924; trans. in L. S. Hsu, *Sun Yat-sen: His Political and Social Ideals: A Sourcebook* (Los Angeles, 1933), pp. 257 and 258.
14. *China Yearbook 1924/25,* p. 863.
15. See Sun Yat-sen's marginal comments on pp. 4-7 of *Tan-ho Kung ch'an-tang liang-ta yao an (Two Important Cases for Impeaching the Communist Party of China)* (Central Control Committee of the Kuomintang, 1927).
16. See Sun Yat-sen's San Min Chu I lectures of August 3 and August 10, 1924, trans. in Hsu, *op. cit.,* pp. 389-440.
17. Sun Yat-sen, *Memoirs of a Chinese Revolutionary* (Taipei, 1953), pp. 102-3.
18. Sun Yat-sen, *Fundamentals of National Reconstruction* (Chungking, 1945), pp. 1-26.
19. Ayub Khan, "Pakistan Perspective," *Foreign Affairs,* XXXVIII, No. 4, 545-56.
20. Information Department of the United Arab Republic, *The Charter* (Cairo, n.d.); cited hereafter as *The Arab Charter.*
21. See, for example, Kwame Nkrumah, *Africa Must Unite* (New York, 1963), pp. 69 and 70, where Nkrumah discusses his concept of a one-party "people's parliamentary democracy."
22. V. I. Lenin, "Democracy and Narodism in China," *Selected Works,* IV (London, 1943), 305-11.
23. Text of Lenin's speech in *Selected Works,* X (London, 1938), pp. 239-44.
24. See Harold Schiffrin, "Sun Yat-sen's Early Land Policy—The Origin and Meaning of 'Equalization of Land Rights,' " *The Journal of Asian Studies,* XVI, No. 4 (August, 1957).
25. Sun Yat-sen, *The International Development of China* (2d. ed. [Chinese and English texts]; Taipei, 1953).
26. *The Arab Charter,* p. 81.
27. *Ibid.,* p. 73.
28. Mao Tse-tung, *On New Democracy* (reprinted, Peking, 1964), p. 42.
29. *Ibid.,* p. 21.
30. *Ibid.,* pp. 36-42.
31. *Ibid.,* p. 42.
32. Text in *The New York Times,* May 24, 1925.
33. Sun's speeches and interviews in Japan, on the occasion of his last trip to Peking, are contained in Sun Yat-sen, *The Vital Problem of China;* see especially pp. 162-73, and 148-54.
34. Mentioned by Sun Yat-sen in his first San Min Chu I lecture of January 27, 1924, as well as in an address to the First National Congress of the Kuomintang; trans. in Sun Yat-sen, *Fundamentals of National Reconstruction,* p. 75.

THE CONTRIBUTORS

GOTTFRIED-KARL KINDERMANN is Professor of Political Science at Munich University and Director of its Seminar for International Relations.

WERNER KLATT is a Fellow of St. Antony's College, Oxford University. He is the editor of, and a contributor to, *Chinese Model*, and the author of the forthcoming study *Land and Labor in Asia*.

RICHARD LOWENTHAL is Professor of International Relations at the Free University of Berlin. During the academic year 1968-69, he was with the Center for Advanced Study in the Behavioral Sciences, Stanford. He is the author of *World Communism: The Disintegration of a Secular Faith*, and of numerous articles on Communism and international affairs.

EMANUEL SARKISYANZ, Professor of Political Science at the Institute for South Asian Studies, Heidelberg University, is the author of *Buddhist Backgrounds of the Burmese Revolution*.

DONALD S. ZAGORIA is Professor of Government and Director of the Research Institute on Modern Asia, Hunter College, City University of New York. He is the author of *The Sino-Soviet Conflict, 1956-1961; Vietnam Triangle: Moscow, Peking, Hanoi;* and the forthcoming *The Social Sources of Peasant Radicalism*.

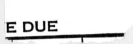

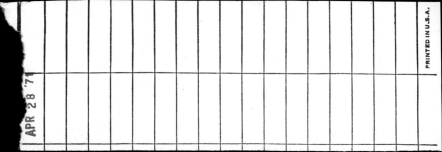